AF326696

WHAT THE HELL IS WRONG WITH MY DOG?

YOU ARE WHAT'S WRONG!

*Understanding How We Create
Our Dogs' Behavioral Problems*

ALISA PETERSON-WHITE

ISBN: 978-1-970435-55-9

Published by: Ink Founders

Publisher's Note:

The stories in this book are true accounts from the author's 35+ years of professional dog training experience. Names and identifying details have been changed to protect client privacy. The training methods described reflect the author's personal approach and experience. Readers should consult with their veterinarian or a professional dog trainer for advice specific to their individual dog's needs.

Contact Information:
Email: alisa.peterson@yahoo.com

TESTIMONIALS/ ENDORSEMENTS

Dr. Troy Pope, M.D.

Jupiter was a bit of a mess when Alisa took over his training. After her boot camp, his change was so noticeable that I decided to make her a regular part of his life by continuing his training. He spends almost two weeks out of each month with Alisa at her facility and has become a mature, intelligent GSD through her methods and training.

Ashlee Mounce, L.P.N.

Australian Shepherd Breeder, Ashlee's Aussies

As a breeder, Alisa and I work closely together with the training of all my litters. I have been to other trainers, but when I found Alisa, I knew she was the real deal. I truly appreciate the knowledge and care reflected in her book. It highlights the importance of proper training and the bond it creates with a dog, something she demonstrates so perfectly.

DEDICATION

To **Papa Peterson**

whose gentle hands and wordless wisdom with animals lit a fire in me that has never gone out.

To **James Waters**

who saw in me what I had not yet seen in myself.

To **my husband, Art**

my supporter, my builder, my heart.

And

To **my mother, Betty June**

you are my one and only perfection.

AUTHOR'S NOTE

Before we begin, I need to be honest with you about something: this book isn't going to coddle you. It's not going to tell you that your dog's problems are all just bad luck or genetics or something beyond your control. Because after 35 years of training dogs, thousands of them, I can tell you with absolute certainty that in the vast majority of cases, *you* are what's wrong with your dog.

Now, before you throw this book across the room, hear me out. I am not saying you are a bad person. I am not saying you don't love your dog. What I am saying is that you probably don't understand your dog the way you think you do. You are treating your dog like a furry human child when what your dog actually needs is for you to be their pack leader. You are projecting your own emotions onto an animal that operates on completely different instincts. And in doing so, you are creating the very problems you're desperate to fix.

I learned to understand animals from my grandfather on his farm in Jackson, Tennessee. He had a gift for reading animals; not just dogs, but horses, cats, even the deer we would sneak out to watch in the early mornings. He taught me to look into their eyes and see their souls, to read their body language, to understand what they were truly communicating. He was tough when he needed to be, gentle when that was called for, but always, always the alpha.

The stories you are about to read are all true. I have changed names and some identifying details to protect my clients' privacy, but every crazy, heartbreaking, hilarious, and ultimately hopeful moment actually happened. These are real dogs and real owners who came to me in desperation, and what I hope you will see in these stories is yourself.

You will probably laugh at some of these owners. You might shake your head at their mistakes. But if you are really honest with yourself, you will recognize something familiar in each story. Maybe you see yourself in the owner who can't leave for work without an emotional goodbye that sends their dog into a panic. Maybe it's the owner who lets their dog jump all over guests because "he's just being friendly." Or maybe it's the owner whose house is being literally eaten apart by a dog who's screaming for structure and discipline.

My approach is direct. Some would say blunt. But it comes from a place of deep love for dogs and a genuine desire to help both dogs and their owners live better, happier lives together. I have cried over these dogs. I have celebrated their transformations. And I have been frustrated beyond measure when owners refuse to do their part.

Because here's the thing: I can train your dog. I can fix almost any behavioral problem. But if you don't change too; if you go right back to the same habits, the same energy, the same mistakes, your dog will regress faster than you can say "sit-stay."

So, as you read these stories, I want you to do something for me: be brave enough to see yourself honestly. Be willing to admit that maybe, just maybe, you have been part of the problem. And then be willing to become part of the solution.

Your dog is waiting for you to step up and be their alpha. They are waiting for structure, for discipline, for someone to help them understand what's expected of them. They want to please you, but they need you to speak their language.

Are you ready to learn?

—Alisa Peterson-White

TABLE OF CONTENTS

INTRODUCTION

WHY DO OUR DOGS ACT OUT?

So, where does one begin? There is so much information that it can be hard to compartmentalize. What I hope to achieve with this book is to get you, the reader, to see yourself within these comical yet serious true stories that I will be sharing with you. If you see yourself along with your dog's problems and you are able to see the constructive criticism at the same time, while finding it somewhat humorous, then I have been successful.

With over 35 years of experience training and understanding dogs, I am confident there will be a story here that resonates with you. I hope these stories create a state of reflection and pensiveness that translates into meaningful change for you and your dog.

Change is the operative word here for everyone. As an owner, you must be willing to change your ideas and rethink what you believe you already know. I promise you, those preconceived notions are likely wrong.

Why are they wrong, you might ask? Because you are not approaching your dog by understanding their instincts. So often, we project our own emotions onto our dogs, believing they think or feel exactly the way we do. This is natural for us as humans, and I do understand, yet it is detrimental to a dog's overall happiness, obedience, structure, and instinctual needs.

For example, if your dog seems sad because you are leaving the house, instead of worrying about it all morning or apologetically telling them how sorry you are, you must be the "alpha" and simply say, "I am leaving." Don't look back and don't cry. Don't go to work and spend the day telling coworkers how bad you feel. If you spend the day upset, your dog will sense that energy when you return home.

This behavior only confuses your dog and creates a state of chaos for them. That is when you see destruction, "potty accidents," or even depression. We honestly put them into a state of mind that is not natural to them; we create negative behaviors along with an unhealthy mental state for our dogs.

If you treat them as dogs and understand their instincts, you will find that your relationship will thrive. Behavioral issues will diminish, leading to an overall happier and more emotionally stable dog.

As you read these stories, I want you to look at:

- The instincts of each dog.

- The natural state of a dog within a feral pack.

- How you might be injecting personal emotions that are not natural to them.

- The need to always be the alpha rather than their equal.

Do not try to be their "Mommy" or "Daddy," and do not treat them like a human baby. Like children, dogs need direction, structure, discipline, and consequences. However, dogs require these in different increments because they possess instincts that children do not.

The Silent Language of the Pack

So many clients tell me that I understand dogs and talk to them in ways others cannot. In the dog world, there is an incredible amount of knowledge that is overlooked, overanalyzed, or completely misunderstood. I focus on the communication between dogs within a pack unit; the innate dynamics that are hardwired into every dog. I listen to them, and often, I already know what they are thinking. Perhaps it is a gift, or perhaps it is simply the result of 35 years of experience.

When you look back at the instincts of dogs, meaning wolves, there is a strict order to everything. Their lives are governed by survival, and they are experts at identifying the "weak link" within the group.

As a child, I watched *Mutual of Omaha's Wild Kingdom*. I saw things that seemed unthinkable in our human lives: tigers taking down antelopes, going for the throat, and tearing out their guts. Those moments were tragic and upsetting, yet I couldn't stop watching. I would get lost in those moments, gaining knowledge about the survival of all animals.

Wolves, of course, stood out to me. They are the closest ancestors to the domesticated animals in the human world. So many things began to click as I watched the order of how they conducted their survival as a pack together. They were a family, a team, and a unit with an unspoken camaraderie.

Let's break this down in the simplest terms possible:

- **The Alpha male eats first**, followed by the Alpha female.

- **The weakest links eat last;** if they try to disobey this order, the Alpha corrects them by holding them down, yet never breaking the skin.

- **They will stand over them** to ensure the correction is accepted until the "Omega" rolls over in submission.

- **When a dog is born with a defect** that is mentally challenging in nature, the Alpha will run that dog off from the pack unit once it comes of age.

- **They are given a chance to survive** on their own, but if the dog tries to return, the Alpha will run them off several times before ultimately killing them to protect the group.

Dogs are survivalists, and if one member brings vulnerability to the pack, they will get rid of the weak link. The thing that was so personal to me while watching this "beautiful dance" was that the pack truly did not want to hurt this dog. They showed hesitation and even dread within the act. They wanted things to be structured without question and didn't want a weak link to create a moment of inferiority.

The Alpha gives them many chances to step up to the challenges and strengthen the pack; it is only after these chances are exhausted that they will kill the weak link. We must understand what is natural to them. They are born with the instinct to survive, but also a natural capacity for compassion and a fierce loyalty to their pack.

They love each other and cry when a member dies. The Alpha will sit by the dead in recognition, howling (crying) for them. The other pack members never howl until the Alpha does. I am still trying to figure out if this is because of the pecking order or if the members are being prompted to show respect.

While I lean toward "the order" when looking at wolves in the wild, we watch our own dogs mourn when a family member passes within our households. So, in this case, our dogs are not being prompted, nor are they following a "pecking order" in that moment; they genuinely grieve the loss of a family member. Wolves are different in the wild because they must have a strict order to survive, but I believe they grieve just as our domesticated dogs do.

Instinct vs. Modern Perspectives

Why did I find this so intriguing as a little girl? Even though I cannot stand watching animals kill or be prey today, watching wolves was mesmerizing to me then. I am deeply passionate about studying the "pecking order" of wolves; I have studied them for over 35 years, and the information I have gained is absolutely invaluable.

Today, some researchers conduct studies comparing domesticated dogs to wolves to understand the differences. Some conclude that dogs are not like wolves at all, claiming they have no instinct or survival skills and are entirely at our mercy. I once watched a special on the Discovery Channel where they tested how dogs mimic human behaviors, such as sneezing. The owner would sneeze to prompt the dog to do the same. After repeating several times, sometimes the dog would sneeze, and sometimes it wouldn't. Was it because they were just mimicking the owner's behavior? It's possible, but I believe it is more of a learned response rather than mimicking. We teach our dogs to sit, lie down, or shake through repetition. We say "shake," take their paw, and give them a treat. After some repetition, they begin to learn what we are asking because they want that treat, right?

* * *

My rationalization and knowledge are rooted in watching feral packs of dogs running wild. Some of these dogs may have been domesticated at one time, while others were born in the wild. I have personally seen various breeds within these feral packs: Labs, German Shepherds, hounds, and terriers.

In these packs, an Alpha male is always established. They hunt together and run off any weak links within their unit. Even if a dog was domesticated at one time, they will return to their instincts when in survival mode. This is why I say: yes, innately, they are still very much like wolves in the wild.

I have never sat in the woods watching wolves in the wild, and I do not pretend to be an expert in that specific field. However, *Mutual of Omaha* certainly enlightened me. Wolves were obviously my favorite; between the ages of 10 and 12, I gained so much from watching them. Since then, I have continued to learn by training thousands of dogs over 35 years. I watch the "alphas" try to take over, and I step in to be the Alpha myself.

I embrace dog after dog that is just searching for direction when they look at me. When we place our emotions into these dogs, they act out. Unfortunately, these dogs need discipline, and we can love them to a detriment. When I speak of discipline, I do not mean spanking. I mean, calling them out on what they are doing wrong. These dogs need the order and discipline that comes from an Alpha.

We often bring them into our world to fill voids in our lives. I see it constantly: single women who treat a dog like the child they never had, or mothers of four at home, will love their dog more and try to humanize them. I ask myself all the time: what is missing in our lives that causes us to put so much emotion into a dog?

Take separation anxiety, for example. That anxiety almost always stems from someone within the family. In their natural environment, dogs don't even know what anxiety is. It simply does not exist in their world or their thought processes.

* * *

My training approaches dogs from the natural world of instincts. Putting a dog into a "down" is the most submissive behavior for them. When dogs jump on you, it is obvious that they lack discipline. I could have five German Shepherds in front of me, and the reasons they jump would all be different: some are dependent, some are anxious, some have learned negative reinforcement, and others are simply demanding attention.

Our dogs are a product of us and what we teach them. If we get a dog to fill an emotional void, we create the dog's issues ourselves. When I train a dog, I gauge my success on how they would survive in the wild with a pack:

- Would they be an Alpha and lead a pack?

- Would they be a hunter in the middle of the pack?

- Would they be the "puppy sitter" while the others hunt?

- Or would they be a "hot mess" that an Alpha would run off or kill?

- Would they be a weak link?

Most dogs, when they first come to me, would be considered "weak links" and would likely be killed in the wild. This is why socialization is so important. I let them run together so they can figure out the pecking order and learn what behavior is acceptable. Sometimes there are tough lessons. If a dog is food-aggressive will get into fights. I step in as the Alpha and correct this behavior before it gets out of control. I make the aggressor eat last! I put them into a "down-stay," so they have to watch the others eat first.

Wolves have an order to everything they do. My own personal dogs are fully trained to this "dog world" standard. Sometimes they try to be Alpha, but then they look back at me to make sure it was okay—because I am the ultimate Alpha.

Dogs need to have a job and work with obedience, especially the working-class breeds. All of your terriers, which might look so sweet sitting in your lap with bows in their hair, still have instincts. Most will burrow out rodents and kill snakes or possums. If we put clothes on them or dye their hair pink, what direction are we giving them? I have watched this mistake being made over and over.

Terriers have major obsessive-compulsive behaviors, along with being extremely tenacious when not worked. They have a strong prey drive and will obsess over lights, lick floors, or turn in circles half the day because they don't have direction. This leads to peeing all over your house, snapping at people, and even biting.

Give them direction with obedience or teach them to retrieve a specific toy. "Go get your monkey. Go get your pig. Go get your blue ball." Work their brains so they have a job to do. If you spend enough time with them, you will see just how smart they are. "Not the red ball, the blue one." It might take several months for your dog to pick up on your command, but with positive reinforcement, they will. They know keywords like "Go," "Ball," "Red," and "Blue," even if they never understand the whole sentence.

For larger breeds, I highly recommend walking them with a backpack. Put bottled water in the pockets and make them feel like they are working. Go through obedience with them for 30 minutes a day. Take them for structured walks where you are leading them, and they are not leading you. This will wear down their energy much more effectively than letting them run in a backyard for hours.

If we humanize these dogs and make them think they are on our level, their behavior will go wrong. If we tolerate them peeing all over our house without repercussions, then we get exactly what we deserve.

Australian Shepherds, for example, are notorious for nipping at hands or heels. Think about this: they are designed to herd by nipping. If those instinctual needs are not met, they will try to herd *you*. They are one of the smartest breeds, and they always seem to want to take over the house. However, once they are given direction and understand their "order" with you, this behavior stops. Time and time again, I witness this; as soon as I correct the dynamic, the nipping suddenly goes away.

But what do we do? We put these dogs in clothes while they chew up couches or pillows. This destructiveness is common with herding breeds and Labrador Retrievers when they lack a job.

You must always research a breed thoroughly before investing money or wasting time. So many clients get a breed they didn't research and then come to me for help, saying, "I didn't know Labs were so destructive," or "I didn't know Yorkies were so spiteful," or "I didn't know Australian Shepherds were so energetic and aggressive."

The truth is, some breeds are just not a good fit for certain households. If you cannot work them and spend the time they require, you need to rethink the breed you are getting. It is as simple as that!

I have written many true stories about this exact issue to help you understand where we fail our dogs. Most are very humorous, and I hope you will enjoy reading them as much as I have enjoyed sharing these encounters.

ENCOUNTER 1

SOPHIE THE HUSKY — PRO BONO

I spoke with this lady on the phone a couple of times before we scheduled obedience classes. We agreed to meet at my facility once a week on Tuesdays at 10 a.m. She seemed like a very nice person and genuinely desperate to get her dog under control.

Our first session was crazy.

Sophie the husky was so out of control that I couldn't get her to listen to anything. She screamed and cried the entire time, desperately trying to run back to her owner. She was so loud that I honestly don't think she could even hear me giving basic commands like *heel, sit,* or *stay.* After just one session, I knew we would never achieve basic obedience through classes alone.

I told the owner I would be willing to keep Sophie for a week to see if I could at least make a dent in her behavior. She agreed and brought her back the following week. This time, her mother and children came along as well; it was a full family event, leaving Sophie in my care for a week. The owner and I spoke for a few brief moments while the kids were saying their goodbyes.

We were all in the garage where I train during the winter. The family walked out to their car. Suddenly, the grandmother barged back in to tell Sophie goodbye one last time.

"Oh, Granny is going to miss you so much! I know you are scared and think we are abandoning you. I know you are mad at us, and Granny wouldn't leave you like this if it were up to *me*, no matter how bad you are! Please don't hate me! Granny loves you more than anything in this world!"

She went on like this for seven minutes.

I finally stepped in and told Granny that she was making it worse. "Sophie is picking up on all of this emotional energy," I explained. "She doesn't know what to do with it. You're better off saying goodbye and leaving." Granny had Sophie standing on her hind legs, front paws wrapped around her neck, hugging her like a human child.

As I watched this unfold, I thought to myself, *This is one of the reasons Sophie is so screwed up.*

I worked Sophie twice a day for an hour and a half each session that entire week. I did not get any obedience commands accomplished. Not ONE! She cried and screamed nonstop, as if I were beating her.

Every time I walked her, she would rear up on her hind legs and box me with her front paws. I was scratched on my face, arms, and legs. I was honestly afraid my neighbors would call the police, thinking I was abusing her.

If I simply *said* the word "sit," she would start screaming.

Needless to say, I had to explain everything to the owner when she picked up Sophie at the end of that week. She agreed that Sophie was psychologically unbalanced and asked what we could possibly do to fix her.

After thinking for a moment, I suggested that once Sophie was spayed, she could come back for my three-week doggy boot camp.

"Oh, I can't afford that," she said. "That's why I was just doing classes."

Out of the goodness of my heart and because I genuinely felt sorry for Sophie, I told her I would do it for free. Sophie was living in an emotionally unhealthy state, and it hurt me to see her like that. The owner was thrilled, and we scheduled Sophie's return for a month later. I asked her to please leave Granny at home. She agreed.

* * *

A month later, Sophie returned; this time with the owner and her neighbor, who drove her.

I took her into the office and had her fill out the enrollment form and sign on the dotted line. While she filled out enrollment paperwork, she began telling me how sick she was. Keep in mind, this woman was only 28 years old.

She started counting on her fingers and rattling off every ailment.

"I have fibromyalgia. I have heart palpitations. I have gained 60 pounds in two months, and no one knows why. I retain too much fluid. I get blinding migraines; that is why my neighbor drove me today, because I could go blind while driving. I have a brain tumor the size of a golf ball, but it is not cancerous. I have major back pain from a car accident. I have carpal tunnel in my wrists. I can't sleep; I may get one hour a night, so I am on medication that doesn't work. I am seeing a psychiatrist because I am having panic attacks, but I think it's just from all my illnesses."

Long pause...

"Well, as a matter of fact, it is so bad that my doctor told me that he didn't know what else to do for me except take me out behind a barn and shoot me!"

I was shocked by everything she told me, and even more so that a doctor would allegedly say something like that to a patient.

My gut instincts are almost always right, and my gut told me that this otherwise young and physically healthy woman was struggling with psychological issues that made her believe she was constantly sick. Possibly hypochondria, along with a personality disorder. It was clear to me that this was her way of getting the attention she felt she needed.

Once again, I found myself thinking, *this is reason number two why Sophie is so screwed up.*

If an owner is constantly dwelling on illness, living in a perpetual *poor me* state of mind, that emotional energy transfers directly to the dog. Sophie was absorbing every bit of it. In the dog world, there are no psychological disorders as humans understand them. Dogs do not comprehend anxiety, nor do they know how to process it when their owners display it daily.

As a result, dogs may become aggressive or develop separation anxiety because they don't know what to do with that energy. They can become highly destructive and emotionally unbalanced.

I assess every dog that comes in for training using what I call a *dog-world scale.* I ask myself: Where would this dog fit within a pack of wolves? Would they be a strong alpha? A caregiver or babysitter? A hunter? A nighttime security guard? Or would they be at the bottom, trying to work their way up in rank?

Do you know what my answer is almost 99.9% of the time?

None of the above.

Most dogs like this would not be allowed in a pack at all; they would be considered a weak link. An alpha would chastise an unbalanced dog and drive it out of the pack to fend for itself. If the dog tried to come back, they would beat them up with a few puncture wounds and reaffirm that they are not allowed in their pack. If the dog tried several times, the alpha would kill them.

* * *

I trained Sophie successfully over the course of three weeks, and she made dramatic improvements. By the second week, all of the crying and screaming had stopped. By the third week, she was performing full obedience like a show dog. I was so proud of the progress she made that I created a before-and-after video. It was remarkable and almost unbelievable. I truly believe that, after her training, Sophie would have become a hunter within a wolf pack.

I scheduled a day and time for Sophie's pickup; however, that morning, I woke up with a severe stomach virus. I called the owner and explained that we might need to wait a day or two because I was literally hugging the toilet. She immediately became angry and said she had rearranged her entire day to pick Sophie up.

I explained that I hadn't finalized her paperwork yet and still needed to demonstrate all of Sophie's obedience commands.

"If I don't show you how to handle her obedience, all of this training will go to waste," I pleaded. "We also need to review the corrections I used with Sophie and go over everything in the paperwork. I am so sorry that I am sick, but we can do it tomorrow afternoon or evening."

She hung up on me.

About an hour later, I received a call from our local detective.

"Yes, ma'am," he said politely. "I have a woman here in my office claiming that you have kidnapped her dog and are refusing to give her back."

"What the hell?" I responded. "This woman is flipping crazy. I trained her dog pro bono just to help her."

I explained the entire situation to the detective. He told me there was nothing he could do and that he had explained the same thing to the owner.

"I completely understand your situation, being sick and needing to go over the training," he said. "But is there any way we can resolve this today? Would you be willing to crate the dog and allow her to pick Sophie up without the training demonstration?"

I agreed, knowing that all of my hard work would likely go right out the window. I also made it clear how unstable this woman seemed.

"Yes, ma'am," he replied apologetically. "I completely agree."

After she picked up Sophie while I was throwing up for the thirteenth time, I texted her and asked why she would do something like this after everything I had done for her and Sophie, especially for free. She never responded.

I have no doubt that poor Sophie regressed right back into her old behaviors and once again became the chastised dog within the pack. I reached out several times over the following months, but to no avail. She never contacted me again.

It was incredibly disheartening as a trainer, as you can imagine. I think about Sophie often and hope she is doing well. But through this experience, I came to fully understand that the problem was never the dog; it was the owners' emotional issues bleeding over onto her. There were simply too many emotions placed on Sophie, leaving her confused and frustrated.

* * *

What Sophie's Story Teaches Us

Breaking this down, Sophie never truly had a chance to become the great dog I helped her become during those three weeks. When an owner thrives on chaos, sickness, self-pity, and hopelessness, and even creates situations filled with conflict, such as claiming their dog is being held hostage, that mental and emotional energy inevitably bleeds over onto the dog and disrupts their natural state of mind.

When we get sick, there is a natural progression that takes place between us and our dogs. They comfort us during times of need and instinctively offer support. Problems arise when we expect more from them emotionally than they are capable of giving. That is when things begin to go south.

Sophie did not deserve the chaotic emotions placed on her. It was similar to a reversed form of Munchausen syndrome, where illness is used to gain attention; except in this case, it revolved around the owner's many ailments, none of which her doctor could find medical evidence for. Eventually, the doctor gave up, reportedly saying, "I don't know what to do but take you out behind a barn and shoot you."

Now I understand why he reached that point. He was frustrated and genuinely did not know how to help her. Medically, everything appeared normal, yet week after week she presented with new symptoms. When this level of emotional instability affects family members, it will inevitably affect the dog as well.

Her mother's excessive emotional display while saying goodbye to Sophie spoke volumes. From the very beginning, Sophie never had the opportunity to simply be a normal dog. It was an unfortunate situation, and I sincerely hope the owner eventually learned to manage her emotions.

As owners, we should never project all of our negative emotions onto our dogs. Doing so only confuses the dogs and can lead to anxiety and aggression. Sadly, I am certain Sophie will spend the rest of her life surrounded by chaos, never fully understanding how to achieve emotional stability.

ENCOUNTER 2

ROTTWEILER AND BAD MOM

I do not work with Rottweilers unless they are under six months old because of the aggression factor. What I dislike about this breed is that you will never see it coming when they bite; it happens out of nowhere.

I once received twelve stitches on the inside of my leg from a Rottweiler bite. I had handed the dog a treat, which he took gladly. As I turned to talk with the owner, the dog suddenly bit me. He clamped down on my inner thigh and refused to let go. The owner had to grab a board and hit him on the head to make him release me.

That's the thing about knowing your breeds: you must be aware of dogs that show no warning before they attack.

Rottweilers were used years ago during the Civil War. They were sent to the front lines to take bullets so that soldiers could advance with their firearms. This breed has always had to be tough without question.

Despite my reservations, I reluctantly scheduled a seven-month-old male Rottweiler named *Tank* for my three-week Doggy Boot Camp. At seven months, I knew the likelihood of being bitten was slim.

The owners arrived one afternoon to enroll Tank. While the wife filled out paperwork, Tank jumped on my pool table five times, leapt on me several times, and even wrapped his paws around her waist, pulling her toward the floor.

This is typical Rottweiler behavior. The breed requires a very strong owner, physically and mentally, to establish themselves as the alpha.

Once the paperwork was finished, the owner immediately began crying.

"I am just going to miss him so bad. I don't know if I can make it three weeks," she said.

I asked, "Didn't you say you have kids?"

She sniffled and replied, "Yes, I have four kids under the age of twelve."

I told her, "Listen, I know you love this dog, but why don't you focus on your kids? Maybe spend more time playing with them while Tank is gone."

To my surprise, she said, "I don't play with my kids. I play with my dog!"

After years of dealing with owners, on this particular afternoon, I snapped. Sternly, I pointed my finger at her and said:

"Then that makes you a bad mother!"

The office fell silent. I swear I heard a cricket chirping from the bathroom down the hall. Even Tank sat down and stared at me as if to say, "*Wow.*"

Her husband quietly walked away, pretending to study the photography hanging on my wall to avoid the tension.

In my mind, I thought: *"Oh crap! I need to get better at censoring myself. She is going to tear up the paperwork and walk out with Tank."*

Remarkably, she did the opposite.

"You are right. I didn't mean that I don't play with my kids. Of course I do. I am just upset about leaving him, but I know it is for the best," she said, wiping away her tears.

She then asked with a smile, "Please let me know how training is going. Is it okay if I call to check on him?"

I replied, "Of course. And if I don't hear from you, I will call you in a few days."

* * *

I trained Tank fully in obedience and was able to redirect his energy from trying to take people down to the ground, to having a job. I would walk him with a backpack, and he loved it.

Believe it or not, the owner rarely called me; perhaps out of respect. She truly was a sweetheart, which made me feel even worse about snapping at her that day.

When the owners arrived for Tank's graduation, I reviewed all his paperwork and then showed them his obedience. He was flawless, and he could have competed in an obedience show ring.

But when the owner tried to work him, it was as if I had never trained him at all or that he had forgotten everything. Of course, he hadn't forgotten; he simply knew he could manipulate her and avoid doing his obedience. After several attempts, with me guiding her the whole way, he finally performed his obedience for her.

About a week later, she called me saying that he had regressed and was being destructive, along with trying to jump in order to pull her down to the floor again. She stated that he was also tearing into the trash and carrying it all over the house. I told her that I would come to her house the next day, and I would try to see what was going on.

* * *

When I pulled into their driveway, I immediately noticed the damage. All the blinds in front of the house were destroyed and chewed. I could see the huge paw print smudges on the windows.

"OMG! Well, let's get in there and see the damage. I have seen worse… I corrected it before… I can do it again," I said aloud to myself, preparing for battle.

I rang the doorbell and stood there looking at the blind that had been shredded on the door. I shook my head and took a deep breath as I heard the footsteps coming to the door.

Her eight-year-old son opened the door and exclaimed, "Thank goodness you are here. Tank has been horrible."

I stepped inside, and from the kitchen, the owner called, "I'll be right there. Let me get Tank inside from the backyard."

Suddenly, the door burst open with such commotion that I thought it had been torn off its hinges. I heard the huge gallop of Tank full steam ahead, taking down everything in his path. His casualties included the smallest daughter, a lamp, a kitchen chair, and another lamp as he rounded the corner.

He was headed right for me, and before I could respond, he had jumped on my chest. As he came down, a nail cut a 12-inch-long gash in my leg.

I immediately took him down, flipping him onto his back and holding him loosely by the neck until his energy dropped. He knew exactly what I was saying to him. I had done this several times during training. He stopped completely.

When I let him up, he shook it off and ran to his owner, jumping on her and trying to pull her down. I stepped in again. I repeated taking him to the floor and holding him.

Released once more, he bounded off the couch, landed in the middle of the coffee table, and grunted at me. I commanded, "Off!" He listened, then came and sat in front of me.

Looking up with those beautiful brown eyes, he seemed to say, *"I don't know why I act this way. I really want to be good."*

I teared up, squatted down, and petted him.

The owner rushed over, saying, "Oh my gosh, let me get some peroxide for your leg gash." She thought my tears were from pain. I quickly told her I was fine.

"Come talk to me and tell me what's been going on," I said.

Before she could answer, the kids chimed in:

- "He broke my new Barbie doll."

- "He chewed up Dad's new chair in the garage."

- "I have a scratch on my arm."

- "Mom has a huge scratch on her stomach."

The little girl added, "Don't ya, Mom? Show her what Tank did."

The owner lifted her shirt, revealing a wound that made my gash look like a paper cut.

"OMG! And what did you do to correct him?" I asked sternly.

She replied, "Well, nothing at the time because I was worried it would get infected. So, I just went to the bathroom and cleaned it really well."

I then asked about the broken blinds. "Did these get broken before training or after?"

The smallest girl answered, "Some...some of them he did before. But he broke these ones and these ones the odder day. And and and come to my room and I show ya how he broke my barbie doll."

I was livid with the owners for allowing Tank to get so out of control again. I had put so much time and effort into his training. What the hell? Why would you pay money for training only to allow the same behaviors you wanted corrected to reoccur?

I told the smallest girl to go get her Barbie doll, so I could show everyone how to correct him again, AGAIN.

While the little girl was retrieving the doll, I asked the owner, "So, how is his obedience? Are you working with him every day?"

She paused and admitted, "Well, I try to, but he won't listen to me at all. It's like he has forgotten everything you taught him. I don't understand what I am doing wrong."

I smiled and replied confidently, "Oh, he has NOT forgotten. He just doesn't take you seriously and doesn't want to listen to you."

She nodded in acknowledgment as the smallest girl returned, holding the damaged doll.

"Seeeeeeee… dis is what he did. He chewed her widdle hands off and pulled her head offted."

I won't go into details, but I put Tank into a down and corrected him. He knew immediately that he had done wrong.

The smallest girl scolded him while I worked:

"Tank, you don't ever ever ever git my Barbies again. You are a bad widdle boy!"

* * *

I then took the mother into the kitchen and sat down with her. We had a long, serious conversation while I asked questions about the dynamics within the home. I explained that it was not fair for the kids to have to live like this. Everyone was afraid of Tank and tried to avoid him, and that was not fair to Tank either.

As we talked, I found out that she was overwhelmed. Her mother-in-law was living with them, she had four kids, a husband who worked day and night, she was dealing with depression, and she had no time or energy left to work with Tank. She was also lonely, and Tank slept in bed with her at night, which would have been fine if he wasn't getting up in the middle of the night and randomly destroying dolls, blinds, and trash cans.

Tank had been an excellent dog throughout training at my facility. The problem was not Tank, but it was the lack of direction, structure, and consistency from the owners.

Once I worked directly with the family and showed them what they were doing wrong, everything changed. Tank fell back into line.

He completely stopped the destruction, jumping, trash diving and performed his obedience perfectly.

I made several follow-up trips to the house to ensure consistency with both Tank and the owners. It was worth it because they now have new blinds that remain untouched and a "widdle" girl who once again has Barbies with hands and heads intact.

This was a total owner error case.

ENCOUNTER 3

LABRADOODLE AND THE CRAZY SCHOOL TEACHER

A woman called me, explaining how much her Labradoodle needed discipline. She told me she had heard rave reviews about my training:

"I do believe that my dog would do wonderful with some direction. A couple of my friends recommended you, so I figured that my dog Harley would do awesome with what you offer."

She was very concerned about not wanting to neuter Harley. I agreed to accommodate her request, provided all the other dogs in training were neutered.

We scheduled an appointment and discussed what to bring for Harley's three-week boot camp stay. She mentioned she was a school teacher and looked forward to learning from me through the training process. She seemed like a great owner and a genuinely good person, teaching children and loving her dog deeply. I was excited about Harley's arrival and the changes I could make.

* * *

The first week of training was tough. Harley was so spoiled that he literally stood up on his hind legs and boxed me when I asked him to sit. He would also stand up on his hind legs and claw my arms, trying to intimidate me.

It was July, and the weather was extremely hot. Harley was miserable, panting constantly. I asked the owner if she could get him groomed. Her husband picked him up and asked about Harley's behavior. I reassured him it was fine, and Harley would settle down, but he needed to be more comfortable physically.

Harley was struggling to acclimate to the fact that I was not spoiling him or allowing him to believe life revolved around him. He retaliated against me on several different levels:

1. **Physical discomfort:** Firstly, he was a mess with his bulk of matted hair and was actively miserable with his constant panting while trying to train him. I knew we had to take care of this first!

2. **Loss of indulgence:** Secondly, I was not catering to his every want and demand. He couldn't understand why I would not simply give in the way everyone else always had.

3. **Social rejection:** Thirdly, he hated the other dogs. Why? Because his owners had made him believe that he was human. He would look at the other dogs as if they were aliens. His eyes seemed to say: *"I am not a dog! Can't you see that?"*

Despite his resistance, I empathized with this sweet guy.

* * *

The second week was a little better. Harley had been groomed, finally rid of the matted albatross weighing him down. Yet he still refused to socialize with the other dogs, and training, well, let's say it was a slow go!

He continued standing on his back legs and fighting me on the sit command. Normally, *sit* is one of the easiest commands to teach. But Harley wouldn't do it for a treat. He would literally turn his head away, snub his nose in the air, and refuse.

I tried sitting on the floor beside him, praising him, stroking him, and letting him know I was trying to help. He leaned away, turning his head as if to say:

"I don't care! I don't need your help! I want to go home where things are easier, and I can have my way again."

Many dogs react this way in the beginning, but within a couple of days, they usually accept the changes and adapt to the new way of doing things. Not Harley. Two weeks later, he was still refusing to accept anything.

* * *

During those two weeks, his owner, the school teacher, kept emailing me, asking how he was doing. Anyone who knows me well knows that I am absolutely honest with owners. I explained the difficulties we were having, but remained positive that he would eventually give in.

"It may take four or five weeks before I can get out of him what I know he's capable of becoming," I told her. "He is eating, drinking, not crying, sleeping well in his crate at night, and although he is not socializing with the other dogs yet, he *is* accepting them. That is a big step for him, and I am proud of him. I just wish he would calm down and stop scratching my arms so badly."

I explained this to her on two separate occasions. Each time, she wrote back about how much she missed him and how badly she wanted her "baby" to come home. I talked her through it with positive energy, explaining how much Harley needed this transformation.

"I don't think I can do without him for four or five weeks. I just don't," she would say.

I held her hand emotionally throughout the process, reassuring her that it would be well worth it.

On one of those emails, more than halfway through the training, she asked me again if things were getting any better. I told her the truth, that progress was slow, but there were tiny changes every day. She asked if he was still fighting me and scratching my arms. Of course, I said yes, being completely transparent with her.

The very next email she sent said, "I am coming to get my baby! I will be there in about 30 minutes."

I immediately responded, telling her that he was fine and that there was no need for him to leave. She never responded back.

I got Harley ready to go home and brought him into the office area in the basement. I was confused by how suddenly she had switched gears on me. I had a strong suspicion that she was going to blame me for the training taking longer than we had originally planned. My gut always tells the truth, and I became anxious, wondering if there was going to be a major confrontation.

I paced the room, and poor Harley watched me as if he were actually concerned. I stopped, smiled at him, and cupped his muzzle in my hand.

"It's okay, buddy. I promise," I reassured him.

He *knew* something was up. He kept looking out the glass doors, as if he were expecting someone. That is when everything became strange and awkwardly quiet.

* * *

Thirty-four minutes later, the owners pulled in with their huge black Chevrolet truck. They didn't park in the driveway like most people would. Instead, they swung in and parked behind my vehicle, blocking me in.

Right then, I felt a confrontation coming based on their energy. I took a deep breath to calm myself. I am usually very good at diffusing situations, but I knew this one was going to be a tough one.

I opened the door with a big smile, greeting them before they even knocked.

"Here's your baby!" I said.

Harley, of course, was jumping and whining with excitement. I stepped back and allowed her to love on him, making comments like, "Aww… he really has missed you. Look how excited he is! There's no doubt he totally loves you all."

I kept smiling, my energy very positive, which I believe threw them off.

While she continued loving on Harley, still refusing to look up at me or acknowledge me in any way, her husband finally spoke.

"So, what's been going on?" he asked.

"Well," I said, still smiling, "nothing on my end other than Harley pushing back on his obedience. That is normal behavior. I didn't want you to feel like you had to pick him up. We are making strides, just slow ones, unfortunately, but overall, he has been doing great."

The entire time, I maintained calm, positive energy.

I couldn't help but notice that she still had her face buried in Harley's fur and would not acknowledge me whatsoever. Then her husband followed up.

"So, what's all this about Harley scratching your arms and standing up on you like some wild dog?" he said, letting out a sarcastic laugh under his breath. "What the hell are *you* doing to cause him to act this way? He has never acted like this at home with us. Can I see your arms?"

I held out my arms, covered in scratches, and said calmly, "That's a very understandable question."

"You are damn right it is," he said with a smirk.

"So, in my twenty-five years of working with dogs, I have come across some that are so spoiled and so humanized that it is extremely hard for them to make changes," I said. "I promise you, I have not done a single thing to him other than not allowing him to manipulate me the way he probably does with you. Other than that, I have done nothing but love him and reassure him."

The entire time I was speaking, I could hear her talking to Harley with her face buried in his fur.

"Honey, what has been going on here?" she whispered to him. "Has it just been horrible for you? I promise I will never leave you like this again. I am so sorry, baby, that I did this to you. I know you are a good boy and would never act like this. Did she hurt you?"

What????

Hurt him???

I immediately went from a one to a ten on the defensive scale. Still, I pushed my reaction aside and continued to reiterate that Harley was simply a product of his environment. I assured them again that I had done absolutely nothing to this sweet boy.

She never once looked up to see my arms. She never acknowledged me or spoke directly to me, not one single time. I promise you, not once. This was beyond weird, and even her husband was beginning to look uncomfortable.

Trying to move things forward, I said, "If you would like, I can come to your house to finish his training. I can offer in-home sessions to complete his obedience. We could do classes once a week."

Her husband asked her what she thought about that.

She never looked up. She never answered.

He finally said, "Well, that might be an option for us, and we will let you know."

I leaned down to tell Harley goodbye, and she immediately stood up and said to him, "Come on, honey. Let's go home."

Her husband thanked me and said they would be in touch. He smiled and seemed much calmer than before. She walked out without ever looking back at me, pulling and guiding Harley out the door. Harley looked back at me as if to say goodbye, or maybe to gloat that he was leaving. To this day, I have never figured out which one it was.

* * *

Three weeks passed, and I hadn't heard a word from them. I emailed the teacher to ask if she was interested in finishing Harley's training. She refused and said she did not like her experience and would never recommend me.

I told her I was sorry she felt that way and offered again to come to her home so she could see how I train and how Harley responded for herself. She refused any further help from me.

I sent one final email assuring her that I had never mistreated Harley in any way. I never received another response.

You would think that would be the end of the story, but it wasn't.

* * *

Almost two years later, after hearing nothing from them, I was tagged in a Facebook post where someone was asking for a dog trainer. Several people commented with my name and contact information. Then suddenly, there it was, for everyone to read.

The schoolteacher commented that she had a very bad experience with my training and told people to message her privately so she could give them all the details.

So, I messaged her directly and called her out on it.

"Listen," I wrote, "I tried every possible way to work with you to complete Harley's training, and now you are going to bash me publicly? That is not fair, especially when I did nothing wrong. You need to mention that Harley scratched my arms to pieces during training because of how spoiled he was."

She said this,

"I didn't see the scratches, so no, I don't believe you."

Really?

Her husband stood right there in my office and looked at them. She didn't see them because she never once lifted her head out of her dog's face while crying over him.

I sent her a picture of my arms. Then, choosing to be the bigger person, I let it go. I never responded again.

Neither did she.

I can only imagine the horrible things she continued to say about me; stories she created inside her own distorted perceptions.

* * *

Just under a year later, I posted on my LCK-9 Facebook page stating that every dog must be spayed or neutered before coming to stay for the three-week boot camp. Almost immediately, her husband wrote a long comment claiming that his dog had not been neutered when he came to my facility and that I had never even asked them about it.

I remember thinking, *Good Lord, here we go with the drama again.*

At that point, I had just about had enough of these crazy people. So, I finally did what I should have done two years earlier; I blocked him from my page.

Then his wife jumped in, stating that I had never asked if Harley was neutered. I responded by posting my call-sheet checklist, which includes every question I ask before scheduling a dog. I highlighted the question: *Is your dog spayed or neutered?*

I explained that I had allowed Harley to attend training without being neutered *because she was adamant that she did not want him neutered.* As long as all the other dogs are neutered, I can take in one intact dog. In other words, I broke my own rule to accommodate *her* needs.

That is when she started writing comments that didn't even make sense in relation to what we were discussing. At that point, I blocked her as well.

Soon after, other people I didn't even know began posting harassing comments. I looked them up, and to no surprise at all, they were friends with the school teacher and her husband. So, I began blocking them, too.

I never have drama on my page, just happy videos of puppies jumping through hoops or learning how to ring a bell to go outside. I am sure my viewers didn't appreciate the drama. And this went on *all day long*.

This behavior alone shows the maturity level of these owners, and she is a grade school teacher? It is no wonder Harley was as messed up as he was. Our dogs, like our children, are a direct product of their environment.

That was the last interaction I ever had with these owners.

* * *

It's been over ten years now, and I still think about poor Harley. When owners humanize dogs, they don't understand how deeply it messes with a dog's psyche. Dogs *are* canines, not humans, so why do we insist on pretending they are our children? Or worse, that they are our equals or even higher in the pecking order than we are?

These are the questions that puzzle me daily, and yet, they are also the very reason my business continues to thrive.

ENCOUNTER 4

ADHD LEONARD

Leonard, Leonard, Leonard — that is all I can say. Leonard was a Miniature Pinscher full of energy, with a love for life that was almost infectious. Training him made me want to get up and approach life with that same positive energy.

His owner called me one day, at his wit's end. He could not do anything with Leopard, and nothing he tried seemed to work.

"When I get home in the mornings, because I work nights, Leonard gets excited and then jumps into the middle of my bed and pees. He chews on everything, along with peeing all over my house. I took him to my mother's one day and he tried to run off, but thankfully I was able to catch him. He refuses to listen to anything I tell him. He actually will do the opposite of what I am trying to get him to do. He jumps all over my furniture, he jumps on everyone that comes in my house and when they sit on my couch, he jumps with pouncing all over them while licking them in the face, head and mouth. I do not want to get rid of the little guy but I can't handle him."

"When I get home in the morning after working nights, Leonard gets excited, jumps into the middle of my bed, and pees," he told me. "He chews on everything and treats the whole house like a bathroom.

I took him to my mother's one day, and he tried to run off; thankfully, I caught him. He refuses to listen to anything I tell him. In fact, he usually does the exact opposite. He jumps on the furniture and everyone who walks through the door. When guests sit on the couch, he pounces on them and licks their faces and heads. I don't want to get rid of the little guy, but I can't handle him anymore."

The owner was a single man in his late twenties, helping run a successful family business. I knew him by name from our phone conversation. He worked constantly to keep the business going, and I suspected that lack of attention might be part of Leonard's problem. We scheduled Leonard for training that week, including the three-week bootcamp. From everything we discussed, it was clear: Leonard needed structure and proper discipline.

* * *

The first couple of weeks with Leonard were a whirlwind. He was into everything and peeing all over the place. My days consisted of constant commands:

"Leonard, would you drop that? Leonard, would you stop that? Leonard, come over here! Leonard, leave that alone! Leonard, stop humping everyone! Leonard, stop taking everyone's toys! Leonard, stop chewing on those cords! Leonard, get off my couch! Leonard, stop jumping! Leonard, go lie down on your bed! Leonard, go lie down! Leonard, go lie down!"

This went on all day, minute by minute. The other puppies hated him because of his high energy and would snap at him, but he didn't care; he just picked on them even more when he wasn't humping them. I began to realize that Leonard had what I believe is selective hearing. He heard me perfectly well, reacted, but made a conscious choice not to listen.

The first week of training and establishing obedience was a huge task. He would sit, but staying in place was always a battle. He might stay for 30 seconds, then dart across the room, hiding under tables, chairs, and desks. Knowing that I would go and retrieve him to do the "stay" all over again, again and again, until one of us gave in. I never gave in, so the process was daunting, but after the first week, he was staying for three minutes.

Leonard still had accidents in the house, but I discovered that they were not just accidents. They were deliberate and calculated methods to get attention. In fact, all of his bad behaviors were manipulations for attention. This reminded me of some of my college studies in child psychology. Negative reinforcement was exactly what Leonard was seeking with his bad behaviors. Where most dogs want is to please and make you happy, Leonard wanted to do bad things to get attention even if it was negative attention.

I analyzed the situation a little deeper and surmised that his owner had been spending all his time correcting Leonard harshly, without giving him any love. This was understandable because, during the first week, I was doing the same thing, minus the harshness. All Leonard had learned up to this point was to act out for attention. His excitement when the owner came home, followed immediately by peeing in the bed, was a huge red flag. When our children are happy and excited to see us, they do not immediately run to do something negative, unless they are seeking negative reinforcement.

So, this was a game-changer for me. I secretly knew what Leonard was trying to achieve. I removed all negative reinforcement.

Every time he actually listened, I gave him praise along with a favorite treat. When he did something negative, I put him in a timeout on his bed. At this point, he had already learned down/stay for about five minutes.

I didn't go overboard verbally when correcting him. In fact, I did the opposite: I put him in a down/stay and completely ignored him the whole time. Occasionally, I would say, "Leonard, did you pee on my floor? Did you chew on that shoe? I cannot believe you did that." Then I would return to ignoring him, with his head down, acknowledging his mistake. It was important that he knew exactly why he was in trouble.

After about five minutes, I would tell him, "Good job! You stayed there so perfectly! What an awesome job you did!" I would praise him and reinforce the good behavior he had just shown by staying and accepting the consequences.

Little by little, Leonard started learning that good behavior was far more rewarding than bad behavior. As he began to understand this, the accidents in the house stopped, the chewing completely stopped, his obedience became amazing, and most of all, Leonard was truly happy with the changes. He performed his obedience with pride and would hold a down or sit for up to 12 minutes. He could hold his urine for three hours and would go to the door when he needed to go outside.

He was still so zestful with life that I sometimes had to tell him, "Leonard, go lay down." He would immediately lay on his bed and patiently wait for the moment I released him so I could praise him. What a fantastic transformation this little guy made in about four weeks. I did have to keep him longer than my program, but it was well worth it.

Leonard also became the "pee police." When a new puppy had an accident, he would come get me, barking and insisting that I follow him. When I did, there he stood beside the accident, proud that it was not his. It was comical, really; although the other puppies didn't find it nearly as funny. I praised him for showing me and made it seem like he was the smartest dog ever. He soaked up that positive attention.

When it was time for Leonard to go home, I dreaded it. You never know how a dog will respond to their owner after training. I knew in my heart that his owner had been too hard on him and was unknowingly undermining what he was trying to accomplish. I scheduled a pickup day, crossing my fingers that everything would transfer successfully.

I made sure to explain to the owner that he had been too harsh. When the owner arrived and walked through the door, Leonard scampered behind me to hide. The owner looked at him and said, "It's me, silly! Don't you know me?" He then looked at me, perplexed, wondering what I had done to his dog. I was a little shocked myself, but I told him to give Leonard a minute.

Leonard finally wagged his tail and crept up to him, as if he was not sure what to expect. He was anticipating harshness, immediately thinking he had done something wrong. Leonard knew what a good boy he could be, but he was unsure whether his owner would recognize it. He did not want to return to his old ways and remained calm, without jumping wildly.

His owner said, "Wow, this alone is worth all the money." Still, I knew this was going to be a struggle for Leonard. I went over the paperwork and correction techniques with the owner first while Leonard ran around, acclimating again to his energy. Soon, Leonard started getting hyper, jumping, nipping at the owner's hands, and grabbing a toy to tear apart. I was sure it was frustration on Leonard's part; here was this negative energy returning, threatening to take away all the good things he had learned.

I showed just how awesome Leonard's obedience was, yet he would not perform it for his owner. I explained to the owner that his personal energy would make or break Leonard's going home and doing well. He appeared to understand what I was explaining, and he left with Leonard, who kept pulling back to look at me as they walked away on his leash.

I was so emotionally pulled in that moment that I went out to his car as he put Leonard inside. I cupped Leonard's face in my hands and told him it was going to be okay. "I promise it will be okay." Leonard was jumping all over the car, restless, as if this was going to be a bad ride to a home he didn't like.

I cried as I walked away, but he was not my dog. He did not belong to me. All I could do was hope that I had successfully transferred the knowledge and understanding his owner needed to be successful.

* * *

Three days later, the owner called me in distress. "He has started peeing in my bed again. He is hyper and jumping all over again. He has not chewed anything because he will drop it if I tell him, at least he learned that. His obedience is not good, and he is running from me when I try to work with him. I don't feel like this training did a thing for him."

I told him that I really needed to do a home visit. Most times, I can spot things I would do differently. I went to his house and found

Leonard completely out of control again. He wouldn't listen to me at all, yet he looked at me as if he wanted me to fix it.

I asked the owner, "So what are you doing to correct him? Are you praising him when he shows good behavior?" He walked me to a door off his kitchen. It led down several steps to a small entrance at the bottom of the house.

"This is where I keep him when he does bad," he said. "I put him down the basement steps because if I try your corrections, he acts out more."

Sometimes, things get worse before they get better. I explained again that secluding Leonard was avoidance. He was not getting the positive reinforcement he needed, sitting at the bottom of the basement steps. He was getting nothing.

"Well, I don't know what else to do," the owner pleaded.

I explained how important it was to actively praise Leonard for good behavior and to never lock him downstairs again. It would take tenacity on his part to show Leonard that he truly loved him. The owner did love Leonard; that much was clear. He just didn't know how to change his own reactions when Leonard acted out. He didn't have the time to invest in Leonard while running the family business, and also did not take to heart what I had tried to explain from the beginning.

* * *

A few days later, the owner called me again, telling me that he was trying to make the changes. Leonard was still acting out horribly, and he felt that he just was not getting anywhere with him. It was time for an intervention, so I told him to bring Leonard back so we could regroup.

Leonard was so excited to be back and immediately picked up where we had left off with his training. No accidents, no chewing things up, and his obedience was awesome. I kept him another week, just following through on his corrections and obedience. During this time, I spoke with the owner several times on the phone, explaining how well Leonard was doing.

"You have to find a way to correct him in a loving and positive way," I reiterated. "Leonard is reacting to your energy, and he honestly is not happy. That is why he acts out with you and doesn't listen."

We set up another pickup day for Leonard, and I was extremely nervous that the situation would go badly and very quickly. Late that evening, around 7 p.m., Leonard's owner arrived to pick him up. He came with his brother and introduced us. He explained that his brother helped take care of Leonard when he was working and that Leonard really loved him.

I went to get Leonard, and he immediately hid. When the brother spoke to him, Leonard wagged his tail and showed excitement. However, he kept hiding behind me, and I could tell the owner's feelings were hurt.

"Let's go out to the garage, and I will show you his obedience," I said, trying to deflect the fact that Leonard was hiding from him. "It's extremely important this time that Leonard does all of this for you before you leave. Last time, I think he just went through the motions, which is why you had issues with him not listening."

Leonard performed his obedience perfectly for me, sitting and staying for over ten minutes. When the owner took the leash, Leonard panicked and laid down on the floor. The owner looked at me in frustration and said, "See! He won't do anything for me."

I told him it was all in his energy and that he needed to be patient. "He knows everything, it's just a matter of getting him to do it for you," I encouraged.

The owner pulled Leonard up by the leash and put him into a sit/stay. Leonard held it for a few minutes, then ran under a nearby chair. The owner looked at me and said, "I am just going to see if he will listen to my brother."

The brother put Leonard into a sit/stay, and he stayed for eight minutes. He then put him into a down/stay for another ten minutes, with me showing him the commands. Leonard did the recall using a whistle, heeled properly, and performed left and right turns. But the entire time, Leonard kept watching his owner, ready to react if needed.

The owner said, "Well, I will keep working with him, and hopefully he will straighten up." I felt sorry for Leonard because I knew he feared being locked in the basement again or corrected harshly.

Leonard went home, and I never saw him again. A couple of weeks later, I called the owner to check in and see how things were going. He told me, "Well, I ended up giving Leonard to an older woman who was looking for a companion. I gave her your information in case she needed you. She has not called you?"

I told him no and asked for her phone number. He apologized for not being able to make things work for Leonard but said he was happy that Leonard had found a good home.

* * *

I called the new owner to see how Leonard was doing and to ask if she needed anything. She told me that Leonard was perfect. No problems with potty training, no chewing anything up, he was doing all of his obedience, and she couldn't be happier. I was so happy to hear this news, and I said, "Well, you know Leonard was not doing well with his previous owner and was acting out with peeing in his bed and refusing obedience."

She said, "Yes, he told me about that. He also said he felt he was too hard on Leonard and that it created a bad relationship. When he brought Leonard to me, he cried. He just wanted Leonard to be happy. I found that so endearing, and I told him I would keep him posted. I actually thought about calling him today. It is so funny that you called me.

"I promise Leonard is doing great and having no accidents in my house. He is not chewing on anything, and when I go to bed at night, he comes to the side of my bed to ask if he can sleep with me. I always let him, but it amazes me that he looks at me and asks. You must have taught him that. You did a wonderful job with him, and I am so glad I have this little guy as my companion.

"When I go outside to check my mail, he walks right beside me and barks to keep anything away. He loves me and barks all the way back to the house. When we get inside, I give him a treat, and the rest of the day is spent with him sitting with me on the couch, eating Cheetos. He loves them and will watch TV as if he understands what they are saying.

"I took him to a groomer last week to get a bath and his nails done, and he did not like it at all! The groomers called me and said he was acting out badly, trying to bite them while they were doing his nails. I told them I would come over and straighten him out. When I got there, he cried when he saw me, and I felt so bad about leaving him. I mustered it up and said, 'Don't you act this way! You have to get your nails done so you don't mess up my furniture.' He calmed down, and with me standing there, he let them do his nails. He is so funny with his actions. I think he just needed me to comfort him. There it is in a nutshell, and I hope I didn't talk your ear off."

She was a very winded woman, and the whole time she spoke, I cried, knowing Leonard had found the perfect home. Throughout the conversation, I knew Leonard was a happy boy. He was protective of her, yet he understood he didn't have to be perfect all the time.

I believe the original owner corrected Leonard too harshly, with spankings and yelling. He didn't give him the positive reinforcement Leonard was reaching for. Eventually, Leonard broke down emotionally and tried to get attention any way he could. I know the owner recognized this and, bless his heart, was willing to find Leonard a better home.

Kids need to know boundaries, what they can and cannot do, and so do dogs. But when you correct them harshly, they will act out. Dogs communicate by urinating on your bed, pooping in your favorite shoe, or tearing things up. If your dog is doing these things, reevaluate the energy you are giving them. If it is constant badgering, rethink it. If your dog poops in your favorite shoe, he or she is trying to tell you something. If your dog becomes aggressive, it is often because of your energy and/or negative corrections.

ENCOUNTER 5

NEED A HOUSE TORN DOWN? CALL 1-800- BEAU!

I once received a call from a woman in total despair. She told me her Labrador had done $10,000 in damage to her home. "My dog, Beau, has absolutely torn down my entire house," she sobbed. I was in disbelief and told her I needed to come see the damage for myself; I needed to see what she was describing.

When I got there, it was unbelievable. Her dog had chewed the siding off the exterior, destroyed the swimming pool until it was non-functional, and dug holes so massive that the owner had fallen and twisted her ankle.

Then she said, "Let's go inside."

Just inside the door, the destruction continued. He had ripped up the flooring, decimated the couch, and literally eaten the walls. I was beside myself, doubting if I could even fix this behavior. I admit I was so overwhelmed by the destruction that I started tearing up. He had chewed her bedroom furniture so badly she'd had to replace a leg on her bed. Her dresser and end tables were destroyed. I am telling you, this was the worst case I have ever seen.

The dog was so hyper that he jumped up and left a huge scratch down the front of my left leg. I still have a scar to this day from it.

My leg was bleeding, and as she ran to get some peroxide, I cried because I was so upset for this dog and this woman.

I sat down on her destroyed couch and asked, "So when is he doing this destruction? When you are home or while you are at work?"

She said, "It's always when I am at work. I come home at the end of the day to find all of this!"

I asked her, "Do you correct him?"

She said yes, she does, with a lot of yelling. "He knows he has done wrong; he goes and hides behind the couch every time. He knows, but he just keeps doing it. What the hell am I supposed to do with this dog?" she pleaded.

I was still crying, apologizing for my emotions. She said, "Honey, it's understandable, because it is devastating to look at for the first time. He is literally eating my house down. That is why I called you; a friend told me how you fixed their dog. Do you think you can fix him?"

I sat there, the couch sinking beneath me, staring at the holes in the walls. I looked from the living room into the bedroom, just trying to process the level of destruction.

I don't claim to have every answer when it comes to these dogs, but this woman needed me to give her hope. I trust my instincts, and I knew I could improve this behavior by at least 85%. I almost always hit 100%, but I like to leave a little room in case something goes wrong.

"I can rehabilitate your dog," I told her, "but only if you are willing to make changes, too. I think you are enabling him, and your corrections are ineffective. Yelling at him is not going to fix a thing; it might actually frustrate him enough to do it all over again. You have to become the Alpha and provide direction. I will teach him obedience, but he needs to come to my facility to learn from the other dogs. It will change everything. Can you do without him for five to six weeks? That is all it will take to fix months of destruction."

She sat in silence for five minutes, rubbing her face. Finally, she said, "No! I can't imagine coming home to an empty house. Not for that long."

What? Did she really just say that to me? Did I hear her correctly?

I shook my head in disbelief. "Excuse me? Are you saying you would rather let your house fall down around you than let him go for a few weeks? You are choosing to be the woman who let her dog chew her home to the ground."

She started to protest, but I kept going. "As upsetting as this destruction is to ME, how can YOU keep living like this? Just because you don't want him away? Because you can't live without him? How can you allow him to keep living this way?"

Tears welled up in her eyes.

"Look at your dog!" I said, my own eyes filling with tears. "Look him in the eye and tell me he is not asking you to help him be a better boy."

Beau laid his head down between his paws, his eyes darting back and forth between the two of us. She scratched the back of her neck in frustration, then let her hand fall against her leg with a loud slap.

"He depends on me," she cried. "What is he going to think when I dump him off at your facility? That I don't love him anymore? That I have abandoned him?"

Now we were getting somewhere! I sometimes have to give these owners tough love to help both them and their dogs. I was standing up for this dog in a way he couldn't for himself.

"You want to know what he is going to think? Nothing! He will miss you at first, I am not going to lie, but my training is deeply structured. We keep them busy sixteen hours a day with training, walking, socializing, and learning games. He won't even have time to dwell on it. I promise! It will only take him a couple of days to acclimate. Once he starts learning a new way to behave from the ground up, he will thank me, just like the others do."

I looked at Beau, and he looked back at me. I couldn't help but smile in a moment of mutual understanding. Deep in my energy, I whispered so only he could hear, *"I am going to help you, Beau. I promise."* He took a sharp breath through his nose, let it out with a small groan, and gave a single kick of his back leg. He whispered back to me, *"Good luck, lady."*

* * *

I left that day, not knowing if she would commit to the training. My last plea to her was, "Listen, I know I was hard on you, but you know you needed it. If you don't get training from me, I will give you the numbers of other trainers who might hold your hand a little more."

She smiled as she closed the door. "Okay, thank you."

It reminded me of those old Charter Ridge Rehab commercials. No matter the content, they always ended with: "If you don't get help from Charter, please, get help somewhere." I was not poking fun at her; I truly meant it.

A week went by, then another, without a word. I figured she had simply resigned herself to the eaten-up house and her destructive dog. Then, she finally called. I did not recognize the number, so I answered, not knowing who it would be. Another Yorkie peeing everywhere, another English bulldog pooping in his crate and rolling in it, another German Shepherd with anxiety and destructive behavior—so who knows what it could be.

I answered the phone and heard these beautiful words: "Alisa, this is Beau's owner. You know, the lab that was destroying my house?"

As if I could ever forget.

"Yes!" I said enthusiastically.

"I have given what you told me some serious thought over the last week or two. You were hard on me, and it broke me down for a few days. I didn't leave the house much that weekend. I sat and looked at Beau, and he looked back at me. Sometimes he would go lick my couch, as if testing me to see what I would do. I did nothing, Alisa, because I just didn't want to deal with it at the time.

"I thought about your warning, about ending up as the poor old lady whose house caved in because of her dog's destruction. I would look him dead in the eye when he came over wanting something. I'd ask him what he wanted, and he would just sit on the floor in front of me. I became frustrated at times and would roll over on the couch, turning my back to him. He would whine and pace around the living room, eventually plopping down on the floor in frustration.

The next week went on as usual, with me leaving for work every morning...

"I came home every day to another new hole in my wall or another shredded spot on the couch," she continued. "I ignored it because I was still too upset to even try yelling at him. I thought about what you said, about what Beau really wanted. Does he really want to live like this? I am broken, Alisa. I stopped yelling because you said it was not working and probably making it worse. So, I just shut up and laid on my couch, ignoring him."

Feeling like a horrible person, I said, "I am so sorry, honey! I promise I was only giving you tough love and sound advice. I was not trying to disrupt your life or break you down. I just wanted to help you both."

Internal panic set in. I thought, *What the hell have I done? Should I just quit training and go back to Psychology?*

"Let me tell you what happened before you apologize," she said. "I was laying on the couch one night, still trying to ignore everything. I was honestly thinking I should find Beau a new home. I was watching TV in the dark when he came up to me again. I told him to please leave me alone, and suddenly, he dropped this clump on my chest. I didn't know what it was, so I jumped up and turned on the light.

There it was, pretty as you please: a piece of drywall he had eaten. I looked him dead in the eye and asked why he did it. You want to know what he said back? He told me, through his eyes and his expression, that he was sorry. I started crying, Alisa, because he finally told me he was sorry. When you made me look into his eyes that first night, I couldn't see it because I was focusing on my own feelings. I saw it this time. I apologized to Beau that night for not loving him enough to fix this. So, I am calling you now. You were right to be tough on me; I needed it. I am ready to bring him in, so let's schedule."

She spoke with such confidence. It made my day in ways I can't express. My elation was so high that I screamed out loud the moment I hung up. "YES!"

* * *

Beau's owner showed up right on time that Monday. I was so relieved she hadn't backed out. I went outside to greet them, and Beau barreled out of the car on his leash, pulling her face-first onto the pavement. She landed on her butt and said, "We are here, and I know he needs this."

I laughed and replied, "Well, let's do some paperwork."

Once inside, Beau was so hyper he leaped over a coffee table, jumped on the couch, tearing down blankets and pillows, and skidded across the floor until he hit a wall. He stopped for a second and immediately started jumping on her.

"I am in full control now," I told her. "You trust me, right?"

"Absolutely!" she said, throwing Beau off of her.

I took him down into a submission. I didn't hurt him, only his pride, but he was a solid 100 pounds. Keeping him in a "down" was grueling. I actually pulled a muscle in my shoulder, but I didn't give up. I held him there for more than five minutes. When he finally calmed, I let go, squatting beside him just in case he tried to bolt.

I looked him dead in the eye, sending my energy straight to him: *Don't even think about getting up.* He didn't move. Ten minutes from start to finish, and when I finally let him up, he didn't jump on her again.

The owner was stunned. "What the hell? Is that all I had to do to stop this?"

"No," I explained. "It takes a certain energy to make them understand. I will teach you all of this once he is trained."

Beau jumped up in the air with excitement, but restrained himself from jumping *on* either of us. His owner eventually left, and Beau watched through the door as she drove away. He cried, jumping on the couch and then running back to the door. He cried again, but then he looked up at me, searching for direction.

I had a treat in my hand and let him smell it. He leaped into the air, almost hitting me. I leaned away and commanded, "Sit!"

He looked at my hand and thought about it, dropping his butt just a smidgen. "Sit!" I repeated, pointing my finger over his head toward the floor.

He sat.

I gave him the treat, and together, we went outside to meet the other dogs.

* * *

To totally transform a dog's behavior is a massive undertaking. You have to start from ground zero and build from there. First, you let them know you are the Alpha, and that is pretty simple, right?

In reality, I have to control everything that the dog thinks, feels, or believes. I have to tap into his brain to show him I am the boss. I immediately start by controlling his food and treats; he only eats after everyone else is finished.

At first, I have to hold him back physically, but eventually, I use only my energy. My trained dogs show him the order of the pack, but I must establish that order myself so every dog understands I am Alpha. I reiterate this constantly to keep the alphas from correcting a new dog too harshly.

I only give a treat if they complete a task or work for it. Whether it is "shake" or "turn around," a "sit" or "down" is always an acceptable task. Changing their feelings is the hard part. If a dog believes a ball makes him happy, and playing a game of "you can't have this," that behavior stops with me.

If they expect to be babied, spoiled, or given special attention, or if they think they can lay on the couch with me, that stops, too. Everything they feel about things changes now.

They try to go back to what they know, but they quickly realize the old rules don't apply here. Spoiling is out of the picture; they realize they have nothing to rely on but Alisa.

Once they reach that state of mind, I let them learn from the pack, and only then. It is a process I don't take lightly. My goal is not to tear down their spirit or mold a brand-new dog that the owners won't recognize; that would defeat my whole purpose. While I am dismantling their old beliefs and ways of thinking, I am doing it to rebuild them. It sounds harsh to some, but it is a true healing process for the dog.

Beau had to go through this process, and he did wonderfully. He would give me eye contact while truly understanding his order with things. He finally had direction, and he loved every second of it.

He chewed up my shoes once during his training and even tried to eat my carpet. But once I corrected him in a way he understood, all of that behavior stopped. I tested him as I do all my dogs by leaving for fifteen minutes, thirty, forty-five, and eventually for hours, just to see if he would regress into destructive behavior before going home. He never touched a thing!

He did great with his obedience and his pack orientation. By week five, I was feeling extremely confident. I called his owner, and we scheduled Beau to graduate that following Monday. She was so excited; she told me it was going to be hard to wait, but since she had waited this long, a few more days would hopefully go by fast. I kind of hated to see the guy leave, feeling like we had been through so much together. However, I knew that when he saw his owner, he would still love me, but be so glad to go home.

* * *

Bright and early at 9:00 AM on Monday, his owner rolls in with a huge smile on her face. Beau had been given a good bath, had been walked, and had already finished an obedience class early that morning. When she walks through the door, Beau just sits and looks at her. Her expression drops, but I reassure her, "Just give him a second."

When she finally said, "Beau, I have missed you," it was like something clicked with the sound of her voice. He took off across the floor, whining and barking. It took him about fifteen minutes to calm down. He jumped in excitement, of course, but she remembered what I had shown her before and corrected him a couple of times.

All that stopped, and we went over his paperwork while he just laid on the floor listening. The next important part was to teach her his obedience and to get him doing it for her, to also go over his dominance exercises and routines. I showed her his obedience first so she could get a visual, and she just gasped. "OMG, I cannot believe that he is listening that well! He is sitting still and lying down without a struggle. I just can't believe it."

She rushed over and gave me the tightest, longest hug. "I truly cannot thank you enough! You are a miracle worker!"

I then had her go through everything as well, and he did excellent for her. He tested her a couple of times on his stays, but he was almost perfect. As she headed out the door, she had her paperwork under her arm and was walking Beau with one hand, without him pulling.

Beau came back to me one last time and sat down at my feet to give me his paw. He looked right into my eyes, and I could hear him say, *"Thank you for helping me!"* Out the door they went together, as happy as any owner and dog could be. I admit I cried as they pulled away, because Beau watched me from the back window of the car until they were out of sight.

* * *

Five years later, Beau has never torn up another thing. She won't have to be the poor old lady whose dog ate her house to the ground. She renovated her house and bought new furniture, which I will admit I was nervous about. I went to check on them about six months later. Her house was patched up and fixed, filled with beautiful new furniture.

Some of her neighbors stopped by while I was there to thank me for helping her and Beau. One neighbor hugged me and said, "I thought this house was going to fall in one day. I really stayed up at night worried about what I was going to do if I woke up to see the house caved in on her. You have truly performed a miracle here."

While that was very sweet of the neighbor to say, I just grinned and said, "It was all Beau! He chose to embrace the changes, and I give him all the credit!"

ENCOUNTER 6

THE GERMAN SHEPHERD HOSTAGE SITUATION

I received a call one day from a super polite man who had desperation in his voice. He explained that they needed help immediately. I asked him what exactly the problem was, and he responded, "Let me tell you! I have a nine-month-old German Shepherd named Moose. He's a good dog—I think? But he is a bully and takes over our whole house. As a puppy, he never acted this way, but as he has gotten older, he has gradually started taking over."

"How bad is it?" I asked. "Is he just jumping on furniture and getting on your counters, things like that?"

"Yes, ma'am, but it is much more than that. He jumps all over us to get his way when he wants something, and my kids are terrified of him. When he gets on the couch, he dares us to move him by growling. If I try to pull him off, he bites my hand. I cannot stop him from grabbing food right off our plates while we are eating.

"In the mornings, I have to put Moose in the backyard just so the kids can get ready for school. They literally have to run to the bathroom and slam the door behind them, then sprint back to their bedrooms. If he is in the house in the morning, he takes their shoes while they are trying to put them on. He grabs the back of their pants or shorts and slings his head around. He nips at their clothes and hands constantly."

He took a breath and continued, "When we get home from school, it is the same thing. The kids hide in their rooms until I can get him outside. I feel really bad for Moose because I want him to be part of the family, but I am afraid he is going to seriously hurt someone. I can't even take him for a walk because he refuses to let me put a collar on him; he just bites and growls like he is going to attack me. Miss Peterson, we are literally being held hostage in our own home. My wife stays home during the day, and she is terrified of him, so she leaves him outside. He bites her hands and jumps up on her; he has scratched her face, chest, and arms. Now, we can't even go into the backyard to play on the swing set because he attacks us out there.

"I heard about you through a mutual friend whose German Shepherd you trained, and they told me to give you a call. Can you help us?" he pleaded.

I took a deep sigh before answering. I had seen this before. It reminded me of Tank the Rottweiler and many others from my past. I dreaded it because I knew the grueling work required to turn a dog like this around.

I looked at my schedule; I was booked solid for the next month. I rolled my eyes at myself, already knowing what was about to come out of my mouth.

"Yes. I can take him this afternoon if you want to bring him."

I get aggravated at myself for not saying no sometimes, but this is why I do this—to help people in really bad situations with their dogs.

"Seriously? This afternoon? Oh my god, thank you! My wife was going to make me get rid of him!" he replied, his relief palpable.

* * *

We set a time, and I spent the rest of the day mentally preparing. In these situations, a trainer must gain the upper hand immediately. I knew I was going to have to take this 95-pound dog down and hold him until he became submissive. I knew he would bite, growl, claw, and twist every which way to get his feet back on the ground. Doing this with a 60-pound Golden Retriever is one thing; they give in quickly. This big guy was going to take everything I had to get him under control.

There is no "Tssh!" or a light tap on the side like you see Cesar do on TV. This is real work, and I dreaded it because I am getting too old to wrestle on the floor. It was summer, nearly 85 degrees, and humid.

And what did I do to prepare?

I put on long sleeves and blue jeans, ready for what was about to come my way.

The owners pulled into the driveway in two different cars. His wife got out of the vehicle with Moose on a leash; he was "lassoed" around the neck without a collar. The husband jumped out of the second car and rushed to help her. Moose was standing on his hind legs, clawing at them, then suddenly dropping to the ground so they had to drag him, all while snapping viciously at their hands.

I decided to have them bring him inside so the new environment would immediately throw him off balance.

I took a deep breath and opened the door.

"Come on in, guys. It's okay. He will calm down when he gets inside."

They reluctantly came in, Moose still jumping, clawing, and snapping.

I asked, "So, no collar like I asked you to have on him?"

The husband let out a frustrated sigh. "He would NOT let me put it on, but I brought it." He held it out to me; a clear "let's see if you can do it" moment.

I took the collar and walked toward Moose. He lunged, perhaps just to smell me, but I moved quickly. I grabbed the leash, snapped it taut, and gave a sharp, "Hey!" He sat down instantly, staring at me before glancing back at his owners. I never broke eye contact. I leaned over him, maintaining a steady, dominant gaze.

He tried to look to his owners for help, but they just laughed nervously. "Don't look at us," they said. "We aren't going to save you."

Without hesitation, I snapped the collar around his neck, slipped the leash out of its lasso, and clipped it onto the collar. I gave another quick correction, never breaking eye contact. Moose bolted away from me, trying to hide behind his owners.

"Well, this is new," they laughed. "He's usually a bully; he doesn't act afraid of anything."

"He is not so much afraid as he is confused by my alpha energy," I explained. "His life has been one big game up until this moment."

I needed to ask them questions so I would know how to approach his training and also teach them what they must change at home.

I looked at the wife. "Are you afraid of him?"

"Yes," she said quickly. "We both are, and my kids are terrified."

He knows that, and that fear is one of the things that allowed him to become a bully. You can never let your dog believe he has power over you, because things go bad from there.

"Are you too afraid to correct him?" I asked.

"Absolutely. He will bite me and fight me when I try to tell him what to do," she replied.

"Did you correct him as a puppy, and did he listen?"

"Yes," the husband jumped in. "But she never followed through most of the time. She babied him to death and gave him his way more often than not. Admit it, you did," he said, looking at his wife.

His wife smiled and nodded her head like a little girl caught being naughty.

"I tried to tell her she needed to be the boss of him, but neither she nor the kids ever listened to me. Now that he is bigger, it is all my fault somehow. He used to listen to me in the beginning. I was the one correcting him," he said, getting animated.

"Honestly," I asked, "did you eventually give up and allow him to take over?"

After a long pause, with the two of them staring at each other, he finally said, "Yes. Ultimately, I gave up trying."

"So, you know, he started out knowing right from wrong. You know he wanted to please you. But with a lack of consistent direction and then quitting on him, this is why we are standing here now. True?"

They both nodded.

"Changes are not just going to have to happen here with Moose. They are going to have to happen in your home and within you as well. Can you commit to making the changes I recommend when his training is over? Because if you can't, you will waste my time and your money."

They both agreed.

They said goodbye to Moose and hurried out, promising, "We will call to check on his progress." They were in their cars quickly and ready to leave his bullying butt behind.

Moose walked to the door and watched them practically run from him. I couldn't blame them, but I did feel a little sorry for the big guy.

I took him straight out to the other dogs so he could acclimate and hopefully calm down in the dog world, with me controlling every interaction, of course. I had braced myself for an all-out battle that first day, but it never came.

Wow. I didn't even have to put on my long sleeves and jeans after all.

But when I started his formal obedience a couple of days later, that confidence would disappear fast, and I would absolutely need them. Deep down, I knew that day was coming.

* * *

After a couple of days of him learning the dog world, and me stepping in several times to keep the others from getting too rough with their corrections, it was time for the real circus to begin.

The first day I went to clip a leash onto him, he took off running all over the dog area. He jumped over other dogs, ducked behind dog houses, and even tried hiding under the other dogs before finally cornering himself under a tree in the far corner. I managed to get the leash on him, started to walk away, and BAM! It was like trying to drag a parked truck.

I turned back to him, "I have treats for you." I said firmly. "But the only way you get them is to come with me. Now."

I let him smell the treats in my hand, and as I started to walk, he began to creep along behind me.

"Good boy," I reinforced.

The moment we got out of the gate, away from the other dogs, the wrestling match was on. He jumped on me several times as I tried to take him down. I managed to get him down, but he clawed and bit his way free, forcing me to let go. Each time, he stood back from me as if he were the king.

I took him into my garage training area while he pulled and rolled on the ground behind me. Once inside, he stopped and looked around. I let him sniff and explore, giving him time to get used to everything that might catch his interest.

Then I went back inside the house and pulled on a pair of heavy work gloves, a long-sleeve shirt, thick pants, and protective pads. One look at him had told me this was going to be a wrestling match.

When I came back out, my employees stopped dead in their tracks and just stared at me. They were fairly new and had never seen me suit up like that before. It must have been startling; most of the dogs we deal with are really sweet and only need discipline and structure.

"If you hear barking, don't pay any attention to it," I told them. "Don't worry about me, and absolutely do not interrupt until I'm done."

They looked at each other nervously. "But what if he hurts you? How will we know? Should we look through the window just to check on you?"

"Absolutely not! You girls have to trust me. I have done this so many times before, and I grow wiser each time. It will be okay." I reassured them.

They slinked away with the puppies they were walking, glancing back at me with uncertainty. As I reached the door, I gave them a huge smile and a thumbs up.

I walked back inside with Moose, and my smile vanished the moment he bolted across the floor. He was panting hard, sensing that something was about to happen, even though I was not completely sure myself how this was going to play out. I looked him dead in the eye and knelt to the floor in front of him.

"Look, I really want to do this the easy way," I said softly. "It is up to you how this goes down. I have treats. Let's make this positive, okay?"

I let him smell the treats again. He postures, hair standing up, and lets out an intimidating snarl. I admit, I always regroup when I see this behavior. I have to read the dog's body language and energy to know whether to approach or to give time. I gave him ten minutes to settle, then said calmly: "Enough with the attitude. I don't have all day for you to try to intimidate me. Let's get to it, shall we?"

I reached down and grabbed the leash from the floor. He lunged at me to bite. Years of experience make me quick, and I slipped away before he could reach me.

I took off with him pulling back, wrestling the leash. He flopped onto the ground, forcing me to drag him, hoping I would give up. I tossed treats on the floor to lure him up, but when that didn't work, Moose came at me like a bull, determined to knock me down. I planted my feet, bracing my forearm, and he bounced backward. He came at me again and again with the same outcome.

Finally, he lay on the floor panting as if he was desperately thirsty, so I got him a bowl of water. He drank a little and then looked up to growl at me again. Without words, I thought: *Seriously? If you want to go, I can go.*

He jumped up to charge once more, and I pulled the leash back to stop him from reaching me, a move that requires more upper-body strength than I unfortunately have. Still, I held him back long enough to figure out a strategy. As he reached me, just before he could jump, I twisted my body to grab the back of his collar and took him down into submission.

I had dreaded this from day one because I knew the kind of physical and mental fight I would undertake. It hurts me to have to go to these extremes with these bullies. *Why?* I asked myself. I don't want this; I am a peaceful person, and I am only trying to help him.

I gripped his collar tighter, leaning over his back so he couldn't get up, and he finally started to give in. He lay there in defeat as I leaned down near his face and whispered,

"I am not your enemy," I told him. "I am the person who is going to help you. Will you allow me to do this for you? I am here because I love you, whether you believe that or not."

He suddenly surged up, knocking me off, still not totally trusting me, and charged again. He leaped at me face-forward, crashing down with force against my arms, chest, and legs, biting at me. This is exactly why I wear long sleeves, pants, and gloves. He was trying to intimidate me, and I knew, from the two days we had worked together, that he was already used to my protective gear and, underneath it all, was ultimately fine with me.

After an hour of this, both of us drinking water as fast as we could during breaks, one of my employees stepped inside cautiously. I was exhausted and hoping Moose would give in soon. His head lifted, and I knew he was thinking she would save him. Frustrated at the slow progress, I heard her say, "Well, I am leaving for the day. Is that fine, and are you okay?"

He lunged toward her, looking for someone to hide behind, and she quickly bolted out the door. Look at us both: I was sweating profusely from the clothes and the struggle, my hair all over my face. He was panting, submissive for the moment. Dirt and dog hair covered me as I jumped up from the floor. "You will stay right here! Got it?" I told him firmly.

He wandered around the room for a moment, and I stepped outside. "I told you not to come in there. All you have to do is clock out, honey."

She said, "I had no idea when you told me you would handle the bad dogs that it would be this bad. I am sorry I bothered you. I was just concerned. This is bad, isn't it?"

I laughed inside myself. I have dealt with so much worse. I did protection training for a while and hated it. No, this is not bad, I thought. "No, it really isn't. I have dealt with many more dogs ready to kill. This dog just wants to intimidate me, so no worries, I promise."

She walked away that night in despair, and I called after her, "I will not work him anymore tonight. Does that make you feel better?"

She smiled and said, "Promise?"

Of course, I promised. I put him up in a kennel for the rest of the night, and I kept my word.

* * *

I thought I would give him time to think and regroup for tomorrow. Needless to say, it got worse the very next day. The minute I got him out to use the bathroom, he stood up and boxed me. After all that time to think, how could he still want to fight me again?

I let him run with the other dogs and gave him more time that day. Later that evening, I brought him out for a walk before we worked. He threw himself on the ground again and refused to get up. I pulled him up and knelt in front of him, just as I had the day before.

"Why are you being so difficult? I shouldn't have to plead with you this hard, and you shouldn't be fighting me. I am trying to help you, silly," I told him.

He refused to walk with me, and as frustrating as it was, I didn't push him. Instead, we went over his obedience again. He stood up and fought me the whole time like a wild horse. Finally, I got him into a down position and held him as I had before. This time, he looked at me, and I knew he was giving in. I held him for about fifteen minutes, and when I let him up, he started to jump and fight, but then decided to just sit down. Now we were finally getting somewhere.

I let him go back out to play with the other dogs, and the next day, he was better and kept improving with each day. He still fought me, but he wasn't trying to bite anymore.

* * *

Three weeks later, he was doing all of his obedience and loving his walks. I was impressed with the changes he had chosen to make. I can guide them, but it's always up to the dog to change.

I called his owners and set up a time to graduate him the following Tuesday. They were thrilled to hear he was doing so well. When they pulled in, Moose was standing at the door watching. He started to whine when he saw them get out of the car. They brought their youngest son, about five or six years old, so he wouldn't be afraid of Moose anymore.

When they stepped inside, Moose wanted to jump up in excitement, but once I said, "Off!" he never tried again. We went over paperwork and discussed the changes they needed to make; most importantly, not allowing him to be the alpha, because that would give him room to regress.

We went outside to review his obedience, and he did terribly. He would not listen to them, though he listened to me. He would sit and lie down but refused to stay for them. Then their little boy walked over and said, "Stay, Moose!" And guess what? He did it for the little boy, but not the parents. How interesting, since the boy had always been terrified of him.

We kept working for an hour, and Moose finally gave in to them. He did pretty well. Not as good as I would have liked, but they promised to keep working with him. I was uneasy about his lack of obedience with them, so I scheduled a follow-up visit at their home a couple of days later. I have to admit, I dreaded it. I felt he might regress with them.

* * *

I reached the driveway, praying things had been going well. I knocked on the door, and the wife greeted me with a huge smile. I stepped inside and sat down at the kitchen table.

"Well, how bad has it been?" I asked, dreading the answer.

"Oh, he has tested us for sure, wanting to get up on counters, trying to jump again. But he has not put his mouth on us once. My little boy can even walk him around the block now. He's not afraid of him anymore. We don't feel like we are being held hostage. When I correct him for trying to get on the counters, he listens. I tell him 'out' and 'off,' and he just leaves the kitchen to lie down in the living room. He is out back right now, and the kids come home from school excited to see him. They can actually play in the yard now. My husband comes home and goes through his obedience every day. I am not afraid of him anymore because he listens to me without trying to bite or knock me down. I even do his obedience after everyone leaves for school and work. We are so happy with his personality now and can't thank you enough."

I was in total shock at how well he was doing. I asked if I could see him, and she opened the sliding glass door, calling for him. He came inside and stopped dead in his tracks. He sniffed me for a moment, then lit up with excitement. I got down on the floor, petting him and loving on him. I grabbed his cheeks and told him how proud I was. He whined and tried to climb into my lap as I held him close.

How amazing that no matter how tough the training had been, he loved me, respected me, and appreciated all I had done for him. I left with a wonderful, fulfilling moment and cried on the way home. We had worked so hard, and the owners were doing their part to keep him from taking over their house and their lives again.

* * *

I wish I could say this was a happy ending. But seven months later, they told me they had to re-home him. Little by little, he had slipped back into his old ways. They were busy and hadn't kept up with the training. He grew aggressive again, and they felt they weren't doing him justice.

The new owner wrote me a message on Facebook, saying he was having the same problems: Moose was aggressive and trying to take over the house. I told him I would work with Moose if he wanted, using the same obedience and corrections I had before. He agreed to bring him by so I could go over everything.

I hoped we could work through his behaviors. I didn't want him to become an orphan, passed from owner to owner. We had worked so hard, and he had made so many positive strides. But I keep reminding myself: training is not absolute. Owners must keep up with it, and they also need to make lifestyle changes. There isn't a magic button that guarantees a dog will never act out again. They need discipline, structure, and obedience every single day.

The new owner kept his appointment with me, and when I saw them getting out of the car, I was surprised to see Moose calm and not pulling on the leash. He had not totally regressed, and I was proud to see it.

They came inside, and Moose immediately remembered me. He started to jump up to greet me, but I quickly responded, "Off." He sat down in front of me, licking my hands. The new owner was surprised and said, "Wow, he never gets off me when I get home like that. I tell him off too, but he doesn't listen to me at all."

We went over his obedience, and Moose performed excellently for me. He resisted doing it for his new owner at first, but after some time, he relented and began following commands. I reviewed all the corrections I had used with him and explained how important it was to work him on obedience every single day. I also suggested ordering a dog backpack for Moose to wear during walks.

"If you fill the backpack with bottled water, it will change the walk," I explained. "It will help trigger him mentally into work mode, and he will feel he has a job."

A couple of weeks later, I called to check in and was told Moose was doing everything I had instructed. He was calming down and listening perfectly. I kept in touch for several years, and his new owner was always extremely happy with him.

This was proof that owners must follow through with training at home in order to keep the transformation intact. I am always proud when I run into owners I have trained for, and they express their gratitude, sharing how their experience with their dog has become positive and fulfilling. They can love and enjoy having their dog as a true part of the family.

Now, we finally have a happy ending.

ENCOUNTER 7

THE BASSET HOUND VS MUZZLE

One day, I received a call from a gentleman who was clearly at his wits' end. He told me he had a Basset Hound named Hank who was "using the bathroom" all over the house, even in his crate at night. The dog was chewing up household items and barking constantly.

He said, "We are about to move into my mother-in-law's house until we sell our own, and I know they are not going to tolerate this behavior. I love my dog, Hank, but something has got to give. He is one year old now, and I know he can hold his bladder. It's like he is acting out and doing it on purpose. I live four hours away from you, but a friend told me you worked with their dog and were very happy with the results. You must be good if people are traveling across state lines to work with you. I am interested in you working with Hank."

I went through my usual list of questions, and we scheduled him to come in for training a couple of weeks later.

Hank arrived around 5:00 p.m. on a Wednesday, full of energy and confidence. He pranced inside and immediately jumped on me, scratching my leg, not a deep wound, but enough to leave a mark.

The gentleman had brought his teenage son with him, and the son had more to say than his father did.

"If Hank is eating and I try to touch him, he tries to bite me," the son explained. "He lunges at me and spits at me."

His father immediately became defensive. "Oh, it's not that bad," he said. "He's just letting you know not to bother his food. He is not being aggressive at all."

From behind his father's back, the boy looked at me and shook his head yes. I smiled at him while the father continued talking.

"If you can transform this stubborn dog, it would be nothing short of a miracle," the owner said. "He doesn't listen to anything, and I know he pees on the floor when he is mad."

Right at that moment, Hank jumped up and bit him between the legs.

The man doubled over in pain and said, "He is just playing."

I shook my head and replied, "So, that was a 'play bite'? I don't think so. You need to stop making excuses for him."

His son quickly said, "See, Dad? He *does* do it aggressively."

I swear, it took everything I had not to laugh. Hank knew exactly what he was doing.

After they left, I took Hank outside to use the bathroom, and he peed immediately. We came back inside so I could enter the owner's information into my computer and file their paperwork. As I was working, I looked over and saw that Hank had lifted his leg and marked my stairs, a couple of walls, and a door. There were pee puddles everywhere.

Since he had just used the bathroom outside for me, I knew this wasn't an accident; he was marking territory, as unneutered males often do. I had explained on the phone that Hank would benefit from being neutered, but his owner was hesitant. He was thinking about studding him out for breeding purposes. I will take in intact dogs under certain circumstances, such as breeding, but in that moment, I realized what a process it was going to be to train him to stop marking inside.

By 8:00 p.m., it was time to put everyone up for the night. I figured I would let Hank meet and interact with the rest of the dogs in the morning. I placed him in a kennel, and he barked, on and off, all night long. I kept going downstairs to correct him using an empty water bottle filled with pennies. It helped temporarily, but as soon as I returned upstairs, he would start barking again.

This was not a good way for us to start out together.

When I went to get him the next morning, he had pooped and peed all over the kennel. He had stepped in it and rolled in it like a pig, yet he was extremely eager to get out. It was an absolute mess to clean up, and I knew he had done it intentionally. Hank did not want to be kenneled at all, but that's part of the process when potty training is involved.

The following night, I placed him in a crate where he couldn't move away from his mess. He peed, but there was no bowel accident. This routine continued for about a week and a half.

I started his obedience training a couple of days later, and he was not having it. He just kept breaking his "stays" over and over. He loved going for walks, but he would pull me something fierce. I also began working on his food aggression. I made him sit and wait while I "ate" first (usually a cracker), and I allowed a couple of other dogs in training to eat before him. Hank ate last. He actually did really well with that structure and tapping into his natural instincts.

About two weeks into his training, Hank decided to try to bite me.

He did not want to go into a down and was not going to stay. Up to this point, he had been fighting me on it, but I would pull his paw out, and he would lay down for me. But on this day, he made it clear he was not going to do it, snapping at me the whole time.

I decided it was time to introduce a muzzle. He hated it, of course. He pouted in his down/stay and refused to even look at me. After about thirty minutes of wearing the muzzle, I removed it. The moment it came off, he immediately snapped at me again. I put him in his crate and left him there for an hour to think about his behavior. He was not a happy camper, to say the least.

Every ten minutes, I would go downstairs and simply show him the muzzle. He refused to look at it. I crouched down and told him that it was up to him if he wanted to change. We could go the easy way or the hard way, but I preferred the easy way.

The next day, he tried to bite me again when I was putting him into a down. So I got the muzzle out again and just showed it to him. After thinking about it, he laid down on his own.

The next day, he tried to bite me again when I put him down. So, I got the muzzle out again and just showed it to him. After thinking about it, he laid down on his own.

He pouted about it, but I praised him, gave him a treat, and loved on him. Then I worked on a few tricks to build him back up. He learned to shake with both paws and to "speak." We even taught him how to play dead, and he was especially proud of that trick. He would yelp with excitement when we got to the fun stuff. He absolutely loved his tricks.

The funniest part? Whenever I asked him to "down," he would lie down and then immediately roll into "play dead," hoping to earn a treat.

It was actually hysterical, and I couldn't help but laugh when he would play dead during obedience.

Eventually, I had to break him of that so he would lie down and stay without turning it into a trick.

For four weeks, he tested me from time to time. His owner would call to see if he was ready to graduate, and I would have to tell him, "Not yet. But we are making progress every day, I promise."

The owner was always very understanding. "No problem," he'd say. "You keep him as long as you think he needs. I want his behavior fixed for sure, so if he has to stay longer, then that's just how it has to be."

Hank ended up staying with me for six weeks before I felt comfortable sending him home. He still challenged me almost up until the end, but every time I showed him the muzzle, he would immediately give in. By the end of his training, the bad behavior had stopped. He remained most proud of the tricks he could do; they were his favorite part of the day.

The day Hank graduated, I truly hated to see him leave. We had made so much progress, and he had developed a deep sense of respect and love for me. His owners piled out of the car after their four-hour drive, ready to smoke a cigarette, while Hank barked and cried at them the whole time.

I had him at my side on his leash while they regrouped from the trip. He kept looking at me, wondering why I wasn't allowing him to run to them yet.

I kept encouraging him: "Hank, just a minute, buddy. Show them how good you can sit and stay."

He would listen for about three minutes before he just had to bellow at them again. I couldn't blame the poor guy; it had been six weeks since he had seen them.

Finally, the owners finished their cigarettes and called for him. When I let go of the leash, Hank bolted toward them, tripping over his own ears and doing a semi-somersault. He howled and cried until he was panting from exhaustion.

Hank performed all of his obedience commands for me and his owners perfectly. I had been worried he might test them the way he tested me, but I think he was actually proud to show off everything he had learned.

His owners were so happy, constantly asking him to sit, down, or stay, and they were amazed to see him hold a stay for ten full minutes straight. Finally, I had to intervene.

"Listen," I explained, "you're going to burn him out if you keep asking him to do this constantly. If you overdo it, he'll start to resent the commands. He only needs to be worked for about thirty minutes at a time, and you need to make sure you're giving him plenty of playtime, too."

The owners finally understood, and soon they were ready to get back into the car and take Hank home.

Everything was great for about two weeks, until I received a call from the owner one morning.

"Alisa," he said, "Hank has done exceptionally well these past few weeks, but little by little he's going back to barking all night in his crate and trying to bite me when I ask him to 'down.' I don't know what I am doing wrong. I have been letting him sleep in bed with me at night because I don't want him waking up my in-laws. I know I shouldn't be doing that, but I don't know how to break him again."

I thought to myself the entire time: this guy has been letting Hank get away with things to the point that the dog was trying to take over the house again. Soon, he would probably start using the bathroom in the house, too.

I started asking the tough questions. "What are you doing when he barks in his crate? How are you correcting him when he tries to bite during obedience? Have you been working with him every day? Tell me the truth; are you intimidated when Hank tries to bite you?"

He was quiet for a second. "Yes," he admitted. "I'm afraid when he snaps at me, so I quit the training as soon as he does it. I have been super busy with my business, so honestly, I have only been working him about twice a week, usually on the weekends. And I didn't know what to do about the barking, so like I said, I have been putting him in bed with us. My wife is sick of him being in our bed every night."

I took a deep breath and tried to stay calm. "Listen, I'm going to get a little tough on you for a second. Hank must be worked every day for thirty minutes without a fault. As he gets older, you can slack off because he won't need the structure as much, but not now. Did you get a muzzle like I told you?"

"Uhhhh, no," he said in a low voice. "I couldn't find one."

I'll admit, I became aggravated, though I tried not to let it show. "You know you can order one online, right? Order a muzzle and use it the very next time you work with him. After that, you should only have to show it to him when he snaps, just like I told you when you picked him up. Do NOT allow him to get the upper hand, or he will never respect you. You have to be the alpha with Hank, more so than with other dogs.

"If he starts barking in his crate, get the empty bottle with pennies in it and slap the front of the crate every time he starts. Catch him the very first moment he begins; don't let him get worked up. You may have to do this over and over for a night or two, but he *will* stop. If you had used that bottle the first time he started barking, you would have stopped the behavior before it got out of hand. Right now, you are not following through with the corrections I explained. You are going to end up wasting your money, and all the time I put in, all because you haven't followed through."

There was silence for about five minutes. For a second, I thought he had hung up.

"Hello? You still there?" I finally asked.

"Yeah, yeah, sorry, I'm just thinking," he said. "You are absolutely right. I promise I will order a muzzle as soon as I get off the phone. I will make a shaker bottle when I get home tonight, and I will work him as soon as I get the muzzle in. I promise! Can I call you if I still have problems?"

I was so relieved to hear him say that. "Absolutely!" I exclaimed.

There were many phone calls after that initial conversation, but the owner stuck with the corrections until he had turned Hank's behavior around. In fact, this owner recently referred two different clients to me. Both of them told me, "Yeah, Hank's owner said he has a totally different dog now. He told us to make sure we follow through with your corrections, and we are more than willing to do that."

I am incredibly proud that this owner took my constructive criticism seriously and turned things around for Hank.

83

ENCOUNTER 8

WHO IS THE TEACHER

I received a call one afternoon from a teacher whom we will call Jane. She had a small mixed-breed dog that the veterinarian suspected was a mix of Jack Russell and Spitz. Both breeds are notoriously territorial with intense personalities.

Jane explained her situation: "My little dog has become the neighborhood terror. We live on a golf course, and he tries to chase all the golf carts. He even jumped on a little old lady who lives below us and pinched her ankle. Although she was very kind about it, we received a letter from the Homeowners Association. It stated that we must keep our dog on our property, or we could be forced to sell our house and move. Of course, I don't want that to happen, but I don't want to get rid of my dog, Chase, either. I need help getting this little guy under control!"

I knew this would be a difficult case because terriers can be true "terrors," especially once they've been allowed to display antagonistic behavior.

I asked my standard intake questions: "Is he neutered? How old is he? How long has he been acting like this? What have you done to correct him so far?"

She answered quickly and then immediately asked, "So can you help me?"

Bless her heart, she was crying by the end of the call, and I was having a hard time understanding her. I immediately focused on calming her down.

"Listen, we will find a way to deal with his behavior. I can't promise we can ever fully remove that personality trait, but we can certainly find a way for you to manage it. These cases are tough because I have to troubleshoot what works best with his specific personality, but I promise you I can get this at least 85% under control."

She calmed down, blowing her nose, and asked how to enroll Chase in training. I told her I wanted to do a home visit first to evaluate his behavior in his natural environment. We scheduled a time for the next day, and I reassured her one last time.

"Don't worry so much. He'll pick up on your emotions, and it may create a situation where his behavior worsens. So, stay calm!"

* * *

The next day, I went out to the house and was greeted by an absolute sweetheart of a woman. She hugged me as soon as I introduced myself.

"Thank you so much for coming over. I have been trying to stay calm, but he went after the little old lady again this afternoon. Thankfully, I was able to call him back before he reached her. I put him in his crate in the garage afterward; let me go get him."

She was gone for maybe three minutes before Chase came tearing down the hallway, elated to be set free. He ran straight past me, then suddenly stopped and turned to growl. Avoiding eye contact, I began asking Jane more questions.

"So, when you say he 'pinched' the old lady on the ankle, did it draw blood?"

"Yes, he pierced the skin, but it was really just a tiny scratch," she explained nervously.

"Well, if there were punctures and blood of any amount, that's a concern. So, when he acts out like this, you just put him in his crate?" I asked, trying to understand.

"Yes, because I don't want to spank him," she reassured me. "I never even spanked my son when he was growing up."

"I am not saying he needs to be spanked," I clarified. "In fact, that could actually trigger even more aggression."

The whole time we spoke, Chase was sniffing my legs and feet, growling low in his throat. Jane looked at me as if silently asking what to do.

I whispered back, "He's fine. Let him figure me out. I don't think he's going to bite me."

She smiled nervously as Chase suddenly took off toward the kitchen for a drink of water. We sat down on the couch in the living room, and I quietly observed Chase's behavior. He was pacing back and forth in the middle of the floor, occasionally stopping to lick the rug.

"He does this all day long unless he is sleeping or outside," Jane said. "Is this normal behavior?"

I laughed softly. "Uhh... no. He is displaying some obsessive-compulsive behaviors. Dogs typically do not develop repetitive behaviors like this if they are mentally healthy. I don't mean that he is 'mentally challenged' or anything," I quickly clarified.

Jane laughed, though her voice still held a note of worry. "Oh my goodness. I'm a special education teacher at the school nearby, but even we don't deal with obsessive-compulsive disorders quite like this!"

"If he is locking in on these behaviors, it can become extremely frustrating for him," I explained. "Does he display any other obsessive behaviors?"

Jane's voice took on a new clarity. "Now that I think about it, he does. Sometimes when the light comes through the windows in the morning, he chases the light reflections on the floor. He will also lick at the floor where the light hits."

I had dealt with obsessive behaviors in dogs before; if left unchecked, they often progress into aggression. I was starting to understand his frustration and why he might bully the old lady or chase golf carts. I told Jane that Chase would need to stay with me for three to four weeks for rehabilitation. I also made it clear that it would likely require a lifetime commitment from her to keep him rehabilitated.

We scheduled for Chase to be dropped off the next day. I was booked as usual, but I knew we needed to flip this behavior as soon as possible.

*　*　*

The next day, when Jane arrived, she was already in tears as she stepped inside. "Are you crying because you are leaving him," I asked, "or because you are happy I am going to help him?"

"Both!" she sobbed.

After reassuring her for nearly thirty minutes and completing the paperwork, she reluctantly said her goodbyes and left.

I looked at Chase as he stood there, staring out while she pulled away, and I thought to myself, *Boy, we have a lot of work to do in three weeks.*

The first thing I did was introduce him to the other dogs. I placed him with the adult dogs rather than the puppies because I was afraid that he might get "hateful" with them. At first, he did not like being with all the bigger dogs, or even some of his own size. But after a few days, he began to socialize.

The breakthrough came when I caught him playing with a little female Beagle I had in training. They chased each other back and forth for over an hour.

Watching a new dog evolve into the "dog world" mentality is one of my favorite moments. It always brings tears of joy to my eyes to see them playing with their peers and finding their place in the pack.

When we started Chase's obedience training, he was awesome. He soaked up the training like a dry sponge does water. Within a week, he was nailing his commands, and his down-stays lasted up to nine minutes. He amazed me with how much he loved to learn. He would do any trick I threw at him: jumping through hoops, rolling over, crawling, shaking with both paws, giving high fives with each paw, and even finishing with a double high five.

Part of his therapy included mental stimulation games. I taught him to pick out balls by color when asked. We also learned how to turn a small push light on and off with his paw. These activities kept him psychologically challenged, and I watched his obsessive tendencies vanish little by little.

* * *

Just after three weeks, he was ready to graduate. I could not have been prouder of his progress. He was actually one of the easiest dogs I have ever turned around from negative behavior.

The real test, however, would be when he returned home and whether his owner would consistently continue the exercises with him.

I decided to take Chase home for his graduation rather than have his owner pick him up. I wanted to oversee his behavior in his home environment and teach Jane how to continue the mental exercises with him.

When we arrived at the house, he was beyond excited to see her. He bolted out of the car and ran straight to Jane, and just cried while showering Jane's face with wet kisses. Once inside, he scurried all over the house to make sure everything was exactly as he had left it, checking his water and food bowls, his toy basket, and his favorite chair.

Jane and I reviewed all the paperwork and the correction methods I had used with him. After Chase had reacclimated to being home, we began demonstrating his obedience work and finished with his tricks. When it was her turn to do his obedience, she had a hard time being firm with him. I gently explained that she was now his alpha and that he needed her guidance.

I related it to her profession. "Your students look to you as their leader and expect you to guide them through the learning process, right? It is the exact same thing with Chase. He needs that same guidance."

That was her moment of clarity. She found her "inner teaching voice," and Chase responded beautifully. We were able to get him to perform his obedience perfectly.

She was amazed at his transformation. When her husband came home, her face lit up.

"Honey! You are not going to believe this. Chase is a totally different dog, well, a better version of himself!"

Her husband sat on the couch and watched as Chase completed his obedience routine for Jane. He just kept smiling, almost speechless. I then showed her how to get him to pick out the right colored ball and how to handle it if he chose the wrong one.

Now, I understand that dogs do not see colors the way we do, but they know shades. I have successfully taught many dogs to distinguish between objects by color. Chase also demonstrated how he could turn the light on when asked and turn it off on command.

Her husband shook his head in disbelief. "Well, I will be darned! I cannot believe that!"

Before I left, I gave Jane one last piece of advice: "He needs to be worked every day. Keep his mind occupied so he doesn't regress into obsessive behaviors. And don't lose your teaching voice with him. Stay firm, and you'll see that he listens."

* * *

Approximately two weeks later, Jane called with an update.

"Alisa, I cannot thank you enough for what you have done for Chase and for us. He has not gone back to his obsessive behaviors or chased the golf carts. He did run over to the little old lady a couple of times, but he just sniffed her and came right back when I called him. He is doing all of his obedience and mental exercises with me every day, and he absolutely loves his tricks.

She paused, her voice full of emotion. "But Alisa, I want you to know—truly, from the bottom of my heart—your teaching has made me a better teacher with my students. I am firmer with them when I need to be, and they respond perfectly. I have a better understanding now of what I was doing wrong. You have changed my life in more ways than I can explain. Thank you… Thank you."

Through tears, I replied, "I am so proud of you for staying true to the exercises and obedience. You have made my day, and thank you so much for sharing that with me." Coming from a teacher, it was one of the highest compliments I could have ever received.

Some cases are easier than others. Some dogs take to structure, challenge, correction, and obedience beautifully. Jane had unknowingly allowed Chase's obsessive behaviors to take control, which led to frustration, and that frustration was surfacing as aggression toward the little old lady and the golf carts. Chase was becoming aggressive because he was frustrated.

Chase was one of the smartest dogs I have ever worked with, and you have to challenge the smart ones, along with keeping them obedient. Simply placing him in a crate was avoiding the behavior, not teaching him how to manage it.

ENCOUNTER 9

TWO GOLDENDOODLES AND 12 KIDS

I have a story that starts in a completely different setting than you would expect. Last year, I was on vacation in the Bahamas with my family. One morning, we decided to walk into town instead of waiting for a taxi, which always seemed to take forever.

The walk was about three miles and took us nearly an hour and a half. Along the way, we also had to take a ferry across the ocean to reach a restaurant someone had told us was magnificent. It did not disappoint. We enjoyed a wonderful lunch overlooking the ocean, and as a vegetarian, I was delighted to find baked macaroni and cheese on the menu. It was one of the best meals I had since arriving there.

After lunch, while we waited for the ferry to return, we noticed beautiful tropical fish swimming along the edges of the water. Their colors were amazing, vibrant blues, greens, yellows, and purples shimmering beneath the surface.

Suddenly, I got a text message. I had received many messages and calls during this trip, most of which I hadn't answered. I stepped away from the mesmerizing fish to check the message in case it was my daughter or son. I opened it and saw a picture of a beautiful Goldendoodle sitting in the front seat of a car. He was gorgeous and looked so happy, his curls blowing in the wind. I responded, "Do I know you?"

It's funny how people will randomly send me pictures of their dogs, or dogs they want to rehome. I am known for finding wonderful homes because of my connections, so I was a little perplexed about why I was receiving the random picture.

We finally boarded the ferry and made our way to the other side, facing another long walk ahead of us. *Ding.* Another text. I almost ignored it, but as we walked, I glanced down at my phone. It was a reply to the Goldendoodle message.

"Yes! I have a Goldendoodle, well, you saw his picture, and I am in need of some training. He is four months old, and I am having major issues housebreaking him. He is highly destructive and very stubborn. A friend from church recommended you; she said she had brought two Shih Tzus to you for housebreaking and obedience. She was so pleased with the results, and I want the same for Boomer. She even told me the cost and what was involved. I am very serious about getting him enrolled."

At this point, my husband was rolling his eyes. We were supposed to be on vacation. Reading her long message had slowed us down, and we were now far behind the rest of our group.

Before I could even respond, another text came through.

"I need your help really badly because my husband is at his wits' end with him using the bathroom all over the house. My sister-in-law also has a Goldendoodle who needs help with basic obedience and follow-through on housebreaking."

I looked over at my fiancé as we walked. He had suddenly found great interest in everything around him, like rocks, fossils, and even the trees. I quickly typed a one-sentence reply: "I am in the Bahamas on vacation right now; can I get back to you next week?"

She replied immediately, full of apologies, saying that would be perfectly fine. Finally, I could get back to the island and the fossils.

* * *

We arrived back home from our not-so-relaxing vacation to find the phone light blinking with 22 new messages. I looked at my husband, Art, and sighed, "Well, here we go again."

He just smiled and said, "This is your baby. I am going to go take a shower." I followed suit, unpacking and putting off my calls until the next morning.

One of the first messages I returned was about the Goldendoodle. Perhaps because I had already seen Boomer's picture, he was stuck in my mind. The next morning, I retrieved her message and called her.

She answered immediately. "Oh, thank God you are back. This house is in shambles over Boomer. He has chewed through my husband's computer wires. He has peed and pooped all over the house. But the kicker was two days ago, my husband got out of bed to go to work and immediately stepped in poop Boomer had left beside his side of the bed."

She must have saved my number to recognize the call. She had a spunky personality, and it was clear she needed help yesterday.

"I am fully booked for a month right now," I replied reluctantly. "We can schedule something for next month."

"No, that is not going to work," she pleaded. "Seriously, I need help before my husband makes me get rid of him. I have been putting him off for a week by telling him you were on vacation. He absolutely will not allow this to go on for another month."

And so, as I often do, I told her to bring him now so we could fix the situation.

Of course, she scheduled for the very next day, and then added one more detail.

"Well, we live two hours away," she said. "It would really help if we could bring both dogs at the same time to save on travel. My sister-in-law's Goldendoodle needs help, too."

"That is going to be very difficult for me," I told her honestly. "I am already full with the number of dogs I can handle. If I agree to this, I need you to stay focused and understand that there is a lot you will have to learn and change as well. This is a collaborative effort. If I go out of my way for you, I need the corrections for both dogs to be on point from you and your sister-in-law. It is a waste of my time and your money if you don't follow through. I am not trying to be harsh, but I am being honest: if I take on two extra dogs I don't have room for, I expect you as owners to make the extra work worth it."

"Of course we will," she promised quickly. "I promise you, we will absolutely do our part."

We scheduled the drop-off for just two days later.

* * *

So here comes Teresa, we will call her that to differentiate between the owners, came barreling into the driveway with two Golden Doodles, their noses pressed against the car windows. She jumps out in a rush, hooking up leashes to both of them, and they immediately drag her inside. My first thought: *"These two are going to need a lot of guidance."*

Goldendoodles can be extremely hyper and often have absolutely no concept of pack mentality. To them, it's all about the "Me, Me, Me" moment. You know that one person from high school, either the head cheerleader or the star football player? Exactly. It was all about them and who they thought they were.

These two pups walked inside with that exact same attitude: *"I'm here, and you should be glad to know me."* I knew right away that I was going to have to take both of them down from their pedestals. The female, Kate, wasn't nearly as bad as Boomer in attitude; I could tell he influenced her.

Teresa scribbled through the paperwork for both and said, "Good luck. I promise Kate is the better dog; Boomer is, quite frankly, an ass. He does things out of spite just to piss us off. If you can't help him, we'll have to find him another home."

She didn't even say goodbye to either dog. Teresa ran a tight schedule; she had to get back home to get the kids off the bus and start dinner. Time was of the essence.

* * *

I sat there with two flamboyant pups, watching as Teresa drove away. They immediately looked at me as if to say, *"Yes, we are here, so where's my pillow to lie on?"*

As I always do, I took them to socialize with the other dogs. They didn't like this at all; I swear, they acted as if they'd get "dirty" if another dog sniffed them. However, after two days of forced socialization, they were playing tug-of-war with a rope and chasing the others around. Once they were acclimated, they did extremely well.

Next came their obedience work; they both did amazing with it. Though Boone could be stubborn, Kate was quicker to get with the program; she didn't enjoy "tricks" as much as Boone, but her basic obedience was noticeably better.

We progressed through the housebreaking process and trained them to hit a bell on the door whenever they needed to go outside. Both adapted well, except Boomer. He constantly tested me, staring me down as he peed on the floor. He was spiteful and acted out when things did not go his way. We worked through this by me calling him out every single time.

Eventually, Boone decided it was simply easier to stop acting out. He had been spending half his day in "time-out" because he insisted on peeing on the floor just to prove a point. That behavior finally stopped when he realized that conforming earned him much more playtime and praise.

Kate, on the other hand, was perfect at everything, though she still had no interest in doing tricks. I got the distinct impression she felt she was better than that kind of thing. *"I don't do tricks because I am too good for those shenanigans. I'm way smarter than that. Can't you see?"* is what I imagine she was thinking. And that was fine, tricks weren't required, and if she wasn't feeling it, so be it.

Despite a few hiccups during training, I felt both dogs were ready to go home. I called Teresa to share the good news and schedule a graduation day.

"So, they are both doing really well?" she asked, her voice filled with disbelief. "They are not having accidents in the house? And Boone is actually hitting a bell on the door?"

"I wouldn't be sending them home if they had not mastered the training," I replied firmly. "Is your sister-in-law coming to pick up Kate with you? It is very important that I show her how to handle Kate's obedience and go over the proper corrections."

"Yes, we plan to come together to save time and gas," Teresa said in her upbeat voice. Should I bring the kids so they can learn what to do as well?"

* * *

I could tell Teresa was an overachiever, always trying to do everything perfectly. I liked her energy and was hoping her sister-in-law would be just as positive.

Just as that thought crossed my mind, Teresa dropped the kicker.

"Now, Sheila is a very reserved person," she said. "She works all the time, so I watch all nine kids while she is at work. I will also be keeping Kate, but she will have her in the evenings and on weekends. Do you think this will confuse Kate?"

I nearly choked. "Wait… nine kids? How in the world are you going to keep up with nine kids *and* two dogs that require your constant attention? Do you think you will even hear the bell if they ring it? Will you have time to go over obedience with them every day?" My voice was laced with incredulity.

"Honey, I am not Wonder Woman by any means," Teresa replied. "But these kids are going to help. We made an agreement when we got the dogs: the kids have to chip in, or the dogs ship out.

That is why I think it is so important to bring the kids when we pick up Boomer and Kate. Don't you?"

I had to admit, I was extremely skeptical. It sounded to me like there would be way too much chaos in that house for the dogs to stay focused on what they had learned. I don't mind admitting that by the day of graduation, I was a nervous wreck.

* * *

Graduation day finally arrived, and I watched as an SUV and a van pulled into the driveway.

"Yep, she brought every one of those nine kids," I muttered to myself. *This is going to be a nightmare trying to go over paperwork and show obedience.* I mean, how were these two hyperactive dogs supposed to focus with kids crawling all over the place? I quickly decided to tuck the dogs away in the puppy room so I could at least get through the paperwork in peace.

I could hear car doors slamming; *slam, slam, slam, slam,* and I wondered if it would ever stop. Did they bring grandma and the husbands, too? I rushed to the door to peek, and sure enough, I counted twelve kids, plus the two moms. Twelve?! This was shaping up to be a total disaster.

I greeted the moms first, and Teresa immediately spoke up: "We brought some of the kids' friends too, because they are at my house all day playing. I thought they needed to learn how to handle the dogs, as well. I hope that's okay."

She must have seen the panic and stress written all over my face because she immediately took control of the room.

99

"Now listen up!" she yelled. "I want everyone to find a seat and *stay there.* I don't want to hear talking, yelling, or complaining. Miss Alisa has worked hard to train Boone and Kate, so we need to stay focused on what she is going to teach us today. Got it?"

The room went silent, except for one lone four-year-old, who was busy scratching a patch of poison ivy on his arm. "But where are the puppies?" he asked.

"They are in the other room, honey," I replied quickly. "I have paperwork to do first, and then I will let them come out to see you."

* * *

Now Sheila was exactly as Teresa had described, extremely reserved and quiet. She carried an air about her as if she felt she was above certain things. She barely made eye contact with me, constantly texting on her phone.

Now, imagine that? No wonder Kate felt she was above doing "silly tricks." It made total sense now; the reason I felt Kate viewed tricks as stupid shenanigans was sitting right in front of me. Am I a dog psychic? Afraid not. Body language is simply the key to understanding people, dogs, cats, or any living being.

I got through the paperwork with Sheila, who was only half paying attention. At one point, I leaned in and asked, "Are you getting all of this? All the training will go down the tubes if you don't know what to do with Kate once you get home." She simply nodded in acknowledgment and went right back to her phone.

On the other hand, the kids were awesome. While we went over the paperwork, they started whispering, and the boys were poking the girls, typical behavior. But the moment Teresa turned to look at them, everything stopped. She clearly had amazing parenting skills and was fully engaged with me throughout the process.

Finally, I went to get Boomer and Kate out of the puppy room. Teresa addressed the kids.

"Listen up! I don't want anyone moving from their seats. If the dogs come up to you, you may pet them. But I don't want to see anyone standing, jumping, screaming, or dancing to get them excited. We have to keep them calm, so Miss Alisa can show us what they have learned. Everyone understand?"

The twelve kids nodded with understanding, repositioning themselves in order to get ready.

* * *

Boone and Kate walked out calmly until they spotted the kids. They immediately scrambled over to lick them and tried to climb into their laps. The kids were remarkably calm, though the lone four-year-old, Daniel, suddenly stood up and commanded, "Sit!"

"What did I say, Daniel? No standing up," Teresa said, a hint of humor in her voice.

I actually managed to get both dogs to perform their obedience drills side-by-side. It was amazing to me that they remained so focused despite the massive distraction of the children. The kids sat perfectly still and eventually asked if they could try the commands themselves. I let the older kids go first, and both dogs performed wonderfully; then, the younger ones took their turn with the same success.

Teresa went through the obedience routine with both dogs without a single hitch. Sheila, however, stayed on her phone the entire time. I couldn't help but wonder if she was truly prepared to be a good owner for Kate.

The kids were absolutely amazing with the dogs, and they seemed to absorb every word I said. As they were getting ready to leave, one of the older girls came up to thank me, even giving me a polite hug. I was so impressed with them overall that I turned to Teresa and said, "You really are Wonder Woman to have these kids under control like this. They are so polite and appreciative that I feel like I failed as a mother myself; my two were never this good!"

As the kids walked the dogs outside and Sheila waited in the car, Teresa turned back to me at the door. "Oh, I am not Wonder Woman at all," she laughed. "I am a redhead, and we take control of whatever situation is in front of us. If I had a drink, I would toast to both of us. Alisa, you are hands-down awesome for what you have done with these dogs. I promise you, these kids will help. We will keep them trained, and if any kid decides to play video games instead of watching them, they will be in time-out for as long as it takes, just like Boone!"

* * *

Those two Goldendoodles ended up doing exceptionally well after going home, particularly because Teresa stayed consistent and kept up the good work with both of them.

When I spoke with her on the phone a couple of weeks later, she said, "Alisa, the kids have been awesome with the dogs. I actually bought a poster board on our way home from your place, and we all sat at the kitchen table the next day to make a schedule: times for training, potty breaks, and playtime with tricks. I realize now that, as much as I maintain structure for all these kids, I was totally missing the fact that the dogs required the same thing. Your help has been a total game-changer here at my house. I cannot thank you enough."

It was clear that allowing the dogs to just run around the house without structure or obedience had caused all the accidents, destruction, and Boomer's spiteful behavior. I always tell my clients that dogs think in ways very similar to children. If your children need structure, rules, discipline, and obedience, so do your dogs!

ENCOUNTER 10

THE VICTORIA'S SECRET GOLDENDOODLE MODEL

From the day I had my epiphany about writing a book, I could not wait to tell this story. I promise you that every part of it is true. I know some of you will not believe me, and that's okay. I have an owner who can back up every word I am about to write.

I received a call from a young woman who was clearly in distress.

"Hi, Alisa," she said. "My name is Jennifer, and I am having major issues with my one-year-old Goldendoodle. She chewed up the frame of my bed last night and destroyed everything in her path. The other day, she got into my school bag and pulled out my eyeliner, lipstick, and foundation. She destroyed them and ate most of it! I took her to the veterinarian, and he said she would pass it in her stool, so I shouldn't worry, but he did suggest that if she is going to eat objects, I should probably keep things out of her reach."

She let out a frustrated sigh. "I am a schoolteacher, and I am always running half-cocked, so I can't always keep up with everything I put down. I just forget and leave things out because I am so busy. But last night was the final straw when she chewed up the bed frame. My boyfriend is so upset; he told me it is either the dog or him.

"Sassy is the best dog in the whole world, I promise, but she has these issues. I need help before my boyfriend gets up and leaves me. One of my coworkers told me about you; she said her dog was doing awesome after your training. She gave me your number, and I hope you can help. I live three hours away, so I'd need to schedule a weekend drop-off if that's okay?""

Of course, I told her we would work it out and that I could absolutely help with this behavior. I explained that it would likely take five to six weeks of training to correct the destruction and impulse issues.

She hesitated. "Well, I really don't want her gone from me that long… but I have to get this behavior under control."

We scheduled Sassy to start training the following Saturday.

"Well, I don't want her gone for that long," she said with hesitation, "but I have to get this under control."

We scheduled Sassy's arrival for the following Saturday.

* * *

When Jennifer pulled into the driveway and stepped out of the car, I thought to myself, *Wow, what a beautiful girl. She was probably a cheerleader or prom queen in high school.*

She walked toward the door with Sassy pulling so hard, Jennifer was practically tripping with every step, her own hair and Sassy's curls bouncing with each tripping stagger. The moment they stepped inside, Sassy immediately launched herself onto me, paws on my chest, claws scraping my shoulder.

Jennifer sighed. "Well, that's what I'm saying. She is such a loving dog, but she is completely out of control sometimes."

I had her fill out the enrollment forms and took copies of Sassy's shot records while the dog got into everything that she could find. She found a bag of dog food I had tucked under the stairs and spilled it across the floor. Next, she "selected" a book from my shelf and dragged it through the mess. Then, she took a detour to the bathroom, raided the trash, and proudly brought a stream of toilet paper back into the middle of the room.

I looked at Jennifer.

"I know!" she said. "That's why we are here. I promise you she is a really good dog most of the time."

I thought to myself, *This is going to be a definite challenge.*

I had no idea just how crazy it was about to get.

After we finished the paperwork and I answered her questions, Jennifer hesitated.

"Ummm... I have one more thing to tell you. I was too embarrassed to say it over the phone. I don't know how to explain this, I don't even know how to say it, and I don't want it to offend you!"

"Honey, you cannot offend me in the least," I reassured her. "Just tell me."

She took a breath.

"Sassy has… a panty fetish."

I blinked.

"She sneaks into my bedroom, pulls open the top drawer of my dresser, and drags out my Victoria's Secret panties. Somehow, she manages to get them over her head and one leg and struts around wearing them. When she gets tired of that, she pulls them off and slingshots them across the room so she can chase them."

She paused, mortified.

"The strange part is, she doesn't touch any of my other panties, just the Victoria's Secret ones. I have scolded her over and over. She will stop for a while, but then she will catch me when I am busy and steal them from the laundry basket. Can you fix this? It's so embarrassing. I will have company over, get distracted, and she will walk into the living room wearing them in front of everyone."

I laughed so hard that I was crying, bent over trying to catch my breath. Jennifer was laughing too, but hers was more of a nervous laugh. I could tell how embarrassing this was for her to admit.

"Well," I finally managed to say, "this is a first for me with the Victoria's Secret behavioral issue, but I can absolutely rehabilitate her from this. No worries, I promise. Did you happen to bring any panties with you so I can correct her with them?"

Jennifer immediately dug into her purse and pulled out a Ziploc bag containing a couple of pairs of panties. "Yes," she said, holding them out. "I brought *'doodle bait.'*"

Jennifer was precious and such a delight to get to know. Even though she was clearly humiliated, I have to admit, I found the whole situation incredibly entertaining; unfortunately, at her expense.

We moved past the awkwardness of the panty handover, and Jennifer said her goodbyes. As she walked away, she called out, "I have heard awesome things about what you can do. I have total faith!"

Sassy stood at the glass door watching Jennifer get into her car and back down the driveway. The second Jennifer disappeared from sight, Sassy slowly turned around and looked me dead in the eye.

Without breaking eye contact, she leapt onto my pool table, grabbed a stack of papers, ripped them to shreds, and tossed them over her head. She jumped down, ran throughout the area, knocking over a chair and a trash can. Then, for the grand finale, she squatted and peed right on top of the papers she had just destroyed.

Looking back now, when she stared me down, she was saying exactly this: *"I am not going to like this, so I am going to tear some stuff up while I am here."*

I calmly walked her to every single thing she had torn up, dragged out, or knocked over, placing her into a firm down position each time. I scolded her and held that boundary for a solid fifteen minutes. Eventually, she walked over to the door, let out a heavy sigh, and laid down while I cleaned up the mess.

As if she were thinking, *"Well… that didn't go like I expected."*

* * *

For the next three weeks, we were locked in a constant battle of wills. I would tell her to *down*, and she would sit. I would tell her to *sit*, and she would lie down. During obedience, she acted as if she understood perfectly; she just chose to do the opposite.

She socialized with the other dogs wonderfully; however, she was a total hoarder and would hide every single toy in the yard so the others couldn't play with them.

In the beginning, she had absolutely no interest in doing tricks. She carried herself with an air of, *"I am not a dog. I am a human."*

In the beginning, she didn't care about tricks. She gave off a distinct, *"I am not a dog; I am a human"* attitude. If another dog slobbered on her beautiful, highlighted golden curls, she would growl and step away while stepping to get away from them. It was as if she didn't want them getting her hair dirty, or like they were the "stinky kids" on the playground.

I knew a lot of that attitude stemmed from Jennifer's own personality. As decked out and pristine as Jennifer kept herself, I could see Sassy following in her footsteps, right down to wanting to wear her pretty panties. Jennifer treated her like a human or a child, rather than the dog she ultimately was. To break the habit, we had several rounds of "baiting" Sassy with the panties and her sneaking to wear them.

I watched in disbelief as Sassy stretched the Victoria's Secret panties over her head, expertly hooking one paw through a leg hole. True to form, she strutted around wearing them as if she were on a runway.

About an hour later, I watched her calmly remove her paw from the leg hole, stretch the panties with that same paw, and slingshot them off her head clear across the room. I have never in my life seen a dog calculate every step of a performance like that.

But I stayed diligent with my corrections. Within the first two weeks, we had reached the point where she didn't even pay attention to them anymore. We were making real progress. Not only was her behavior improving, but Sassy was actually enjoying herself, shaking, high-fiving, and even jumping through a hoop.

Her obedience was still a little inconsistent, but by the fourth week, we were able to finish up her basics.

By the end of her training, she was wrestling with the other dogs, getting dirty without growling about her curls, sharing toys instead of hoarding them, and behaving like a well-adjusted young lady.

I called Jennifer with the good news.

"Sassy is still your same Sassy-doodle," I told her, "just a much better version of herself."

* * *

Jennifer picked Sassy up on a Saturday afternoon and brought her mother along for the three-hour drive this time. They were both so excited to see her that I had to bring their energy levels down a notch before I even brought Sassy into the room.

"Now, remember," I cautioned, "she is immediately going to try to regress to the behaviors she knows work with you. Do not encourage it, and absolutely do not allow her to jump. The calmer you are, the calmer she will be."

They agreed and did an excellent job keeping themselves composed.

When Sassy entered the room, she started whining softly and crawling low to the ground, rolling partially onto her back so they could rub her belly. The second Jennifer stopped rubbing her and stood up, Sassy tried her signature pounce to the chest. Jennifer corrected her exactly as I had directed, and Sassy stopped instantly.

We allowed Sassy to calm down for about ten minutes before moving on to the paperwork. I went over all the corrections that I did with her, specifically focusing on how to maintain the boundaries around her "panty fetish." For twenty-five minutes, Sassy lay on the floor, perfectly calm and showing no signs of her usual deviance.

Jennifer looked at me, then at her mother. "I cannot believe she is being this good and this calm. She has never stayed still this long."

Her mother quickly added, "She's never stayed still *at all*!"

I went through all the obedience with Sassy, showing Jennifer exactly how to do everything, demonstrating every command and hand signal. Then, I handed over the leash.

"Now," I said, "you have to make sure Sassy does this for *you*."

Sassy tested her, as most dogs do when their owners return, but by the end of the session, she was performing beautifully, even holding a sit for ten full minutes. I was so proud of both of them, because it was hard for Jennifer to stay firm, but she did it. And Sassy seemed proud to show her just how good she could be.

When it was finally time for them to leave, I knelt down to Sassy and told her I was going to miss her. She lifted her paw for me to shake, gently touched her nose to mine, and then turned around to walk out.

It was a very typical Sassy attitude.

She wasn't about to let me know she would miss me. A polite paw shake and a nose touch were more than enough before she busted out of there.

* * *

A week later, Jennifer called with an update.

"Alisa, she is totally different, but in a good way. She hasn't torn up a single thing. She lets me take a shower without crying outside the door. She hasn't jumped on me or anyone else. But the best part? She hasn't touched my panties. I've left them on the floor, hanging out of my drawer, even in the laundry basket, and she just walks by them like she doesn't even know what they are. My boyfriend is absolutely thrilled!"

A month later, she called again.

"Sassy is still doing awesome. She started testing us a couple of weeks after being home, but I did the corrections exactly like you showed me, and it stopped. I cannot thank you enough."

Then, one year later, Jennifer surprised me with a message on Facebook, including a few pictures of a happy, mature Sassy.

"Sassy is still doing great!"

This case was a perfect example of how an owner can unintentionally create behaviors by not providing structure, consistent correction, and clear obedience expectations. But it also shows something even more important, that change is absolutely possible when the owner is willing to grow alongside the dog. Jennifer was able to reel those behaviors in and provide the mental stability Sassy so desperately needed.

I am still so proud of both of them.

ENCOUNTER 11

LABRADOR HELD HOSTAGE

Early in my career, about five years in, I believe, I received a call from an elderly woman about a Bichon. She told me her two-year-old male was terrorizing everyone who came through her door by biting at their ankles and feet. I opted to go to her home to evaluate the dog myself and see just how bad it really was. We scheduled the visit for two days later in the afternoon.

When I pulled up to the property, I couldn't get over how beautiful the house was. The driveway seemed to go on forever, lined with beautiful, blooming pear trees. It must have been springtime.

As I stepped out of my car, I was greeted by two gorgeous blonde Labs. They were incredibly friendly and more than happy to soak up as much petting as I would give them.

I walked up to the door and rang the doorbell. On the other side, I could hear the immediate sound of a small dog barking and scratching the door. Finally, the woman came to the door and opened it.

"Hi, I am Alisa, the dog trainer you called. I am at the right house, correct?" I said, while watching the Bichon lunge at my feet from inside.

"Oh, yes! Can't you tell by this crazy dog barking and trying to bite your feet?" she responded with a laugh.

I stepped just inside the doorway and completely ignored the dog. Instead, I focused on chatting with the owner about her beautiful home. After a few moments, I told the owner, Sue, that I was going to start walking towards him.

I looked her dog, Max, dead in the eye and said, "Enough!" very sternly. I took one firm step toward him, and he immediately ran off into the living room.

Sue looked at me, stunned. "Well, that has never happened before. Let's go inside and see where that booger ran off to."

* * *

We entered the living room, but Max was nowhere to be found. Sue went through the house, hollering for him in the kitchen, the bathroom, and the bedroom. As she came back down the hall toward the living room, she stopped.

"There he is! He is hiding under the darn couch. Max, come out of there right now!" she demanded.

Max didn't budge.

Sue asked me to have a seat and see if he would come out on his own.

"He has never acted like this before. Why do you think he is hiding from you?" she asked, genuinely confused.

I explained that my energy was giving off a dominant presence to him, and when he realized he couldn't intimidate me, he simply didn't know what to do.

Sue called for her husband to come into the living room. As he stepped into the room, she started laughing.

"Can you believe Max is hiding under the couch like this? Please tell her what he normally does so I don't seem like a liar."

He paused, smiled, and said, "Oh, he would absolutely be jumping all over her and trying to eat her feet without a doubt. Hmmm… this is definitely not like him. I think you have him bluffed." With that, he turned and walked back through the house.

"See? I told you he is normally aggressive with everyone, I promise," she pleaded.

"I have no doubt," I said, reassuring her. "I saw his behavior when I rang the doorbell and stepped inside."

After about ten minutes, Max finally crawled out from under the couch and ran straight to Sue, hiding behind her legs. She just laughed and laughed, telling him he was a crazy dog.

Max would look at her, then look at me, clearly confused. Eventually, I was able to walk over and pet him for a few minutes. Before long, he was my best friend, jumping into my lap as I settled back into the recliner.

* * *

We spoke about his behavior for about thirty minutes. I even went out the front door and rang the bell again, trying to elicit a response from Max.

Nothing.

He was smart enough to know I was the one ringing and refused to react.

I explained to Sue that basic obedience classes would not be enough to correct Max's behavior. He would need to come to my facility for doggy boot camp.

Sue sighed and called for her husband to come back into the room.

"She says that Max will need to stay at her facility for three to four weeks in order to correct his behavior. What do you think?" she asked him.

Her husband tugged at his pants, pulling them up around his waist, and looked at me.

"How much money are we talking about?" he asked.

When I told him, he smiled.

"Well, that's not bad at all. I think it is money well spent if you think there's hope for him."

I reassured them both that I could handle the task without a doubt. They agreed to bring him to my facility the following week.

* * *

Monday morning came quickly. Before I knew it, Sue, Max, and her husband, Gerald, pulled into my driveway in a new white van.

Max jumped out, with Sue holding tightly to the end of the leash. Gerald stepped out of the driver's seat, and they immediately walked over to the fence, admiring all the dogs.

I went out to greet them at the gate, noticing how captivated they were by the pack.

"Is the black Lab a training dog?" Sue asked.

I smiled. "No, she's my dog, Isabelle. A very good friend of mine, whom I met while training his chocolate Lab, bought her for me. I have had her for about three months, and she is such a good dog."

"Oh, she is just beautiful," Sue said warmly.

I took them inside to complete the usual paperwork, and they said their goodbyes to Max.

As they were getting back into their van, Sue stepped back out, petted Isabelle one last time, and walked back to my door. I opened it before she could even knock.

"Did you forget something?" I asked.

She shook her head. "No… but I do have a question."

She hesitated for a moment before continuing.

"Would you consider allowing Isabelle to come stay with me while Max is in training? My Labs would love having her, and I would too. It would really help me not miss Max so much if I had her to entertain me and my other dogs."

I pondered the request for about ten minutes. I trusted this seemingly honest, sincere woman, and I didn't see any harm in it. Eventually, I relented and allowed Isabelle to go stay with them.

And that… is where this story takes a turn into a situation so crazy, I could never have made it up, or even imagined it happening.

* * *

Max's training went exceptionally well. His obedience was almost flawless, and all the aggressive behavior had dissipated to nothing more than an occasional small growl. With a simple verbal correction, Max would immediately settle and allow strangers to pet him. I was very pleased with his progress and knew that, with the right guidance from his owners, he would go home and do amazing.

I spoke with Sue several times throughout Max's training to check on Isabelle. She always told me Isabelle was doing great; that she loved all the land they had, running and playing with the two Labs.

"Alisa, she sleeps in the recliner with me in the evenings while we watch TV," Sue told me. "She is just so loving and easy to take care of."

What struck me, though, was that she never asked about Max. At times, I felt she was becoming too attached to Isabelle, but I brushed it off. *Well, she'll get Max back and forget all about Isabelle,* I told myself. Maybe I was just trying to make myself feel better, because your gut never lies to you. And my gut was whispering that she was going to have a hard time giving Isabelle back.

But she would have to bring Isabelle back to get Max. She would never abandon Max or would not want him back.

Right?

Wrong.

I called Sue to tell her that Max was ready to graduate.

"Great!" she said.

Then there was an awkward silence.

"So," I prompted, "what day works for you to pick up Max and drop Isabelle back off?"

Silence again. Then, I heard her whispering to Gerald in the background. I couldn't make out what she was saying.

"Are you still there?" I asked.

"Yes, sorry. We were just trying to figure out a good day to pick him up. Can we do next week on Wednesday?"

I was stunned. It was Tuesday.

It was going to take her over a week to drive across town to pick up her dog?

"No," I said calmly. "He is ready now. If you leave him an extra week, I will have to charge you for that. You live just across town; why don't I bring him to you and go over everything?"

More silence and the sound of the phone being shifted around. Finally, Gerald got on the line. "Hey Alisa, we will be there tomorrow around one. Does that work?"

"Yes, that's perfect. I will see you guys then," I said with excitement.

* * *

One o'clock came and went. Then two. Three. Four.

I called them to see what was wrong. No answer.

Eight and nine p.m. passed without a word. Finally, at around ten p.m., I called again. Sue answered as if nothing were wrong.

"Alisa, I am so sorry. Some things came up today, and we were not able to make it. We are planning for tomorrow at ten a.m. Would that work for you?"

My patience was gone.

"If you do not come tomorrow morning, I am going to have to go to the county attorney's office and file suit," I said, my voice firm. "I do not want to do that, but you are avoiding picking up Max, and

119

that is so sad for him. You also have my dog, and I am looking forward to having her back. My other dogs miss her, and I miss her."

There was another long pause, followed by the familiar sound of whispering. Then Sue's voice came back, but the "sweet old lady" was gone.

"Yes, well, go ahead and file," she snapped. "Because I am not giving Isabelle back. She is part of the family now, and my other dogs are too attached to her. You can keep Max. Sell him if you want, so you can get back the money your friend spent on Isabelle. **I AM NOT GIVING HER BACK!**"

For a moment, I couldn't even process what I was hearing.

What is happening right now?

I will admit I was naive; this woman had completely snowed me. But in all honesty, But if I am being honest, I saw it coming in our conversations. I knew better the moment I agreed to let her take Isabelle home. My gut had warned me.

I thought about poor Max. A dog who had just completed training, who had done everything asked of him, only to be abandoned. The only home he had ever known had been ripped away from him.

How does someone just stop loving a member of the family that they had loved and cared for over two years? Apparently, three weeks with Isabelle was enough to cancel out two years of love?

I was livid. Absolutely livid, and I wanted my Isabelle back

Yes, it was my fault for trusting her. I told myself that over and over. But I was not going to allow my dog to be held hostage.

Not without a fight.

* * *

I said to her, "Soooooo, you are not giving me my dog back, and you are abandoning Max? What kind of person does that? Everything I trusted about you was a lie!"

Gerald grabbed the phone.

"I can't change her mind, Alisa. You are going to have to get Isabelle back legally. I am so sorry for this. I have tried to talk her out of it, but she is not going to budge."

I thought quickly.

"Gerald, if you are not for this, couldn't I just come drop off Max with you and pick up Isabelle?"

I heard a heavy, defeated sigh on the other end. "It's not that easy, Alisa. She is obsessed with Isabelle, and I have to live with her. I am sorry, but to keep the heat off me, you are going to have to legally get Isabelle back."

I hung up.

And I broke down.

I started crying because I didn't have the money to hire a lawyer. I was only five years into my business and just barely breaking even. They knew that. They knew I couldn't afford a legal fight.

Desperate, I called my friend Mark, who had bought Isabelle for me. After I explained everything, "You still have the papers on Isabelle, right?" I asked.

"Yes, I do!" he said firmly. "I will go to my lawyer tomorrow morning."

Thank goodness he was willing to fight this and had the money to do it.

Possession is nine-tenths of the law. I knew we were going to have a battle on our hands.

* * *

The next day, Mark called and asked me to come to the lawyer's office to give my statement. I dropped everything, jumped in my car, and headed straight there.

When I arrived, the receptionist brought me back to a conference room.

"So, this is the famous dog trainer Mark speaks so highly of," the lawyer said, reaching out to shake my hand.

I laughed nervously and sat down.

"What I need from you," he continued, "is for you to tell me exactly what happened."

So, I walked him through the entire story from beginning to end. When I finished, he leaned back in his chair.

"Now, why exactly did you let this woman take your dog?" he asked. "I mean, the story sounds a bit crazy, if you know what I mean. Do you commonly let your dogs go home with people to ease their worries?"

"Of course not!" I replied quickly. "But I truly trusted this elderly woman. She reminded me of my grandmother or something, I guess."

I tried to defend what was obviously a flawed character analysis.

The lawyer laughed.

"You can never trust the 'sweet old lady' thing. I have seen some crazy things with elderly clients. They can be extremely manipulative and play the grandma card to get exactly what they want."

"Obviously, I made an extremely bad judgment call, and I know that now. But what can we do to get Isabelle back?"

He replied, "First, we file a suit against her for theft. We also have Isabelle's registration papers, which prove ownership. She may hire a lawyer to fight this, so we need to move quickly."

And that's exactly what we did.

After she was served with papers demanding the return of Isabelle, she hired a lawyer. Thankfully, once her lawyer reviewed everything with ours, he agreed that the dog needed to be returned.

The county attorney ordered the sheriff's office to go to her home, demand the return of Isabelle, and return Max to her at the same time.

What happened next sounded like something out of a movie.

When the sheriff demanded she hand over Isabelle, she became hysterical. She fell to the floor in the doorway, crying uncontrollably. Eventually, she relented and handed Isabelle to the sheriff, screaming as she did.

But it didn't end there.

As they placed Isabelle into the back of the cruiser, she ran and jumped into the car after her, wrapping herself around Isabelle.

"I won't let her go! You can take me to jail!" she shrieked.

And that is exactly what happened.

She was arrested and spent two nights in jail.

I have no idea what happened to Max. He was handed over to her husband, and I can't even imagine the trauma that poor little dog went through during that exchange.

I never saw this coming, and to this day, I still cannot fully wrap my head around that crazy grandmother. What was she thinking when she climbed into the police car after Isabelle?

The deputies tried to pull her out, and they managed to get her out once, only for her to jump back in to clutch my dog. It was the craziest situation I have ever been involved in.

* * *

A couple of years later, my lawyer told me he had become known as "the lawyer with the crazy dog case." He laughed about it, but I felt bad that his peers teased him over it. Despite that, he remained my lawyer for years until he and his sixteen-year-old son were tragically killed in an airplane crash. That's a whole other story.

Isabelle eventually went back to Mark, and I only saw her when he would bring her by for visits. Each visit brought back all the memories of the craziness that we went through to get her back. Over time, Isabelle became a wonderful companion for Mark's grandchild and, to this day, she is doing awesome.

But I still ask myself: Why did this woman form such an extreme emotional attachment to Isabelle? She already had her two beautiful Labs. She had Max. How does someone simply stop loving a dog they had for two years? How do you shut down your care for one soul and go completely over the top for another?

I don't know if I will ever understand it.

I still wonder about Max. I truly believe his issues stemmed from Sue's emotional state; I believe she created the very behaviors she claimed to hate. When he was with me in training, all those hateful behaviors vanished. He was the most loving and congenial dog. I loved him, and it was so fulfilling to watch his transformation.

That experience changed me.

I learned a massive lesson through that heartbreak. I will never, under any circumstances, allow someone to take one of my dogs "on loan" again.

ENCOUNTER 12

AUSTRALIAN SHEPHERD NEEDS TO BE WORKED

Just a few months ago, I received a call from a wonderful lady whom I will call Peggy. She was at the end of her rope with an Australian Shepherd she had rescued. I will call the dog Maggie.

Peggy was in dire straits over this Aussie and had actually suffered numerous contusions and abrasions from Maggie. She had also been bitten several times, leaving deep puncture wounds in her hands and arms. Yet, despite all of that, she continued explaining how much she loved this dog.

I finally asked her, "What could there be to love about a dog this aggressive?"

"She really is the sweetest dog I have ever met when she is calm," she answered without hesitation. "She sleeps with me every night and lies at my feet while I watch TV. She walks with me to the mailbox every morning to protect me from other dogs and people passing by. The dog pound actually stopped by the other day and asked if I had an aggressive dog. Of course, I told them no, she just barks at people and other dogs to protect me. But when they asked to see her, she lunged and snapped the moment she was let out of the house. That's why I am calling you. She needs training, or they told me they would have to take her from me."

I couldn't allow that to happen to such a sweet lady, so I agreed to take Maggie in for training.

* * *

A month later, I met Peggy and Maggie for the first time. Maggie dragged this poor woman through the door of my office, then immediately turned around and jumped on her, scratching her arm before barking at me incessantly.

I walked right up to Maggie, clapped my hands in her face, and followed it with a sharp, "Hey!

She immediately sat down and let out a low murmur of a growl.

"Wow!" Peggy exclaimed. "I need to learn how to do that!"

I laughed and reassured her that I would teach her how to be more dominant with Maggie by the time the training was over. After filling out the paperwork, Peggy cried as she left my office, looking back at Maggie as if she were leaving her in prison.

I reassured her that Maggie would be just fine and that I would take wonderful care of her.

"I... I... know," she stammered. "I am afraid she will think I don't love her and that I am giving her away."

No one knows for certain what dogs think, but I am of the mindset that they do not think in those layers of processes. Time is not the same for them as it is for us. However, as soon as Peggy pulled down the driveway, Maggie looked up at me with an expression, as if she was agreeing with her mom.

I quickly turned her around and took her through the building. By the time I weighed her and set up her kennel, she was acting as if nothing had happened; jumping on me, scratching my arms, nipping at my hands, and barking again.

Perfectly normal.

* * *

Maggie's training was a struggle at first, but within a week, she was performing her obedience like show-ring material. I was incredibly impressed by her intelligence and her eagerness to learn.

Two weeks into training, she was no longer jumping, nipping, scratching, or barking at strangers, as long as I gave her a verbal command. She had truly become the sweetheart Peggy had sworn she could be.

By week three, she was not perfect, but she was darn near flawless.

When graduation day arrived, Peggy was absolutely enamored with the changes in Maggie. She didn't jump, scratch, nip, pull on the leash, or bark at her. Maggie was a very "vocal" dog who liked to protest and let everyone know her thoughts, so training her not to verbalize every single impulse was a huge feat.

Maggie had always been very verbal, quick to protest, and let everyone know about it, so training her not to verbalize every thought was a huge accomplishment.

But the biggest surprise that day was not Maggie.

It was Peggy, hobbling in with a cane. She was in her seventies, but when she had dropped Maggie off, she had been mobile and agile.

"What in the world had happened?" I asked, stunned.

"Oh, I had a hip replacement while Maggie was in training," she replied casually.

I was flabbergasted. How was she going to work Maggie every day? How would she correct her when needed and follow through with everything Maggie had learned? When I brought this up, Peggy simply shrugged.

"I figured she would be all fixed, and I wouldn't have to do anything with her," she said.

Really?

I was overwhelmed by the lack of understanding, or perhaps the lack of memory. I had explained to her on the phone and again at drop-off that she would have to work Maggie every single day. She would need to walk her. She would have to follow through with corrections. I had even told her that if she couldn't reinforce what was taught, she would be wasting her money and my time.

At the time, she had said, "Oh yes, I understand."

Not to mention, I even have it printed on my office wall:

"Training starts here; success ends with you!"

Where had that conversation gone the moment she left my property?

Nevertheless, sending Maggie home felt like doing so on a wing and a prayer with my fingers and toes crossed.

About two weeks later, I received the call I had already anticipated.

"Alisa, she has gone back to her old ways," Peggy said, sounding defeated. "In some ways, she is worse than before I brought her to you. She is knocking my granddaughter down, whom I have full custody of, and biting her when she gets her on the ground. I can't really correct her because I am moving slow with this hip, and by the time I get to her, it's all over. What am I supposed to do?"

Just as I suspected.

I told her I needed to do a home visit to assess the situation for myself, and we scheduled an appointment for the following week.

* * *

I traveled forty-five minutes to reach Peggy's house on home-visit day, dreading the drive because I honestly felt there was not much I could do.

As I drove, I replayed the conversation in my mind, exactly how to tell her that Maggie might be better suited to someone who could handle her, or perhaps to a farm where she could truly herd. I kept thinking Peggy would be happier with a Shih Tzu or a Yorkie instead.

The dread during that drive was tormenting me.

Now I have to preface this next part with something very important:

Every single event I am about to tell you truly happened. This goes at the top of my list of the most unbelievable yet incredibly true stories.

I knocked on the door and was immediately greeted by chaos. Banging. Running feet. Dogs barking. And a high-pitched squeal from a little girl. Peggy finally opened the door with her beautiful smile.

"Did you hear the scream from my granddaughter?" she asked.

130

Yes. Yes, I did.

"I know it was loud," she continued. "When you knocked, my granddaughter ran over to grab Maggie by the collar to keep her from getting out the door. Well… Maggie bit her hand, and she ran off to her room crying."

I looked down and saw Maggie backing away from the door, staring at me dead in the eye. She started barking and growling as if she had never met me before. I stepped inside, claiming the space and backing Maggie deeper into the living room.

I put my hand out gently. "Now you know exactly who I am! Why are you barking and acting this way? Shhhhh… It's okay, Maggie."

I squatted down to her level. She crept toward me, allowing me to pet her just once before she immediately backed up again, barking nonstop.

I observed her for about five minutes, stood up, and said to Peggy, "She is not barking because she doesn't recognize me. She is barking in protest. She knows I am here to correct her behavior today. What a smart girl she is!"

Peggy laughed and said, "I believe that. She is so smart that she lets herself out of the house and runs all over the yard. She comes back five minutes later, but I wish I could teach her to shut the door behind her sorry butt."

I couldn't help but laugh because I could see that scenario so clearly in my head.

Then I scanned the room.

A middle-aged woman stood by the fireplace, an elderly man sat in a recliner, completely unresponsive to the world around him, and Maggie was lying down, still barking under her breath.

Suddenly, a little girl with a red, pissed-off face came running around the corner toward Maggie, her arm raised in the air. She slapped Maggie on the head and yelled, "NO! You are so bad, Maggie! I hate you!"

Maggie's ears pinned back, and she dropped her head. Amazingly, she didn't retaliate; she just took the correction and lay there.

"Alisa, this is my granddaughter, Amber," Peggy introduced quickly.

"Nice to meet you, Amber," I replied calmly. "But you know, you really shouldn't be slapping, hitting, or kicking Maggie. It could make her behavior much worse, and it certainly is not a nice way to correct her."

"I don't care! She is mean to me too!" Amber screamed back, tears filling her eyes.

"Do you see what I am dealing with here?" Peggy asked.

Through all of this, the elderly man never responded; he just stared blankly at the television screen.

The middle-aged woman never moved an inch, simply watching everything unfold in silence. Peggy never formally introduced her and only referred to her as "Mee Mee." I was not sure if that was her real name or a nickname, but she never spoke a word the entire time I was there. She just observed, quietly lingering in the background wherever we moved.

It was… odd, to say the least.

Finally, curiosity got the better of me, and I asked Peggy who the gentleman in the recliner was.

"That is my husband," she said softly. "He suffers from a very rare, debilitating disease. He can't speak or really engage anymore. He hasn't spoken in over a year or more. He just sits there and watches whatever we put on the television."

What a terrible existence for this poor man, I thought.

Meanwhile, Amber was doing nonstop handstands in the living room during all this conversation. I felt irritation rising. MI was going through menopause at the time, and it didn't take much for me anymore

"Amber, must you do handstands in the living room? You should go out in the yard so if you fall, the ground will be softer than this hardwood flooring," Peggy blurted out in frustration.

Amber stopped for a split second to look me over, then went right back to her endless handstands.

Peggy sighed. "She was diagnosed with ADHD last year when she was five. She never stops moving."

* * *

"Well, let's get to it," I said, wanting to get things moving. "Amber, I need you to go outside and run around the yard so I can see exactly what Maggie does to you. I can't fix it if she doesn't do."

Peggy, Amber, and I walked out to the front yard, with Maggie darting everywhere, jumping on everyone except me, of course.

Peggy prompted Amber to take off running through the yard, and Maggie immediately chased after her.

Within seconds, Maggie knocked Amber to the ground and began nipping at her back, legs, and arms while Amber screamed bloody murder.

I ran over, clapped my hands, and gave a sharp "Leave it!" Maggie stopped immediately and ran back up onto the porch.

Peggy looked at me and said, "I do that, but she does not listen to me."

"Are you doing it from up here on the porch?" I asked.

"Yes," Peggy admitted. "I can't get down there fast enough to do it."

I ran through my thoughts, back to the drive, rehearsing how I was going to explain that she didn't need this dog.

But I started with the injury factor first.

"You know, if this continues to escalate, Amber could get injured, possibly even maimed. Maggie could scar her face, take out an eye, or sever an artery one day."

Peggy nodded in agreement and followed with her own ideas. "I could give her away, I guess, but I love Maggie so much. It would be devastating for Amber, too. She is tough on Maggie, but Amber treats her like a little sister. They play video games together, have tea parties, everything."

"Wait... exactly *how* does Maggie play video games?" I asked, confused.

"Well, she doesn't really," Peggy admitted. "But Amber just puts the controller in front of her and pretends."

Suddenly, I understood.

Sometimes I can't see the forest for the trees, as they say.

Amber had now recovered from her "attack" and was casually picking bloomed weeds out of the yard as if nothing had happened. I asked her to run again and promised I wouldn't let Maggie knock her down this time.

She started to take off reluctantly. "Stop! Let me get down there to you first, okay?" I yelled.

As I walked down into the yard, I glanced back at the porch to make sure Peggy was watching. That's when I spotted Mee Mee standing in the corner of the porch watching me. She had been there the whole time, and I had not even known she was there. It unnerved me, but I was there for Peggy, so I ignored it.

"You ready?" I called out to Amber.

She nodded. Off she ran, with Maggie instantly on her heels.

I took off running, clapped my hands, and gave a sharp "Leave it!" Maggie pulled a hard U-turn and bolted in the opposite direction.

"See, Alisa, I can't do that with my hip," Peggy called down. "And Mee Mee is in natural, non-induced liver and kidney failure, so she can't either. Obviously, my husband can't."

I sighed in frustration as an idea surfaced, one I rarely pulled from my files.

"Peggy, what do you think about a hand-held correction collar?" I asked reluctantly.

"You mean a shock collar?" Peggy exclaimed.

"Yes. A shock collar. It's the only other thing I know to do at this point besides finding her a more suitable home. This way, you'd only have to push a button to correct her. And I really do think it will work." I said with deliverance.

We walked back up onto the porch, and I asked Peggy to head inside.

"Amber, you need to come inside, too!" Peggy yelled.

"No! I don't have to. Why don't you try and make me!" Amber dared, flipping back up into a handstand.

Peggy led me back inside, sighing. "She will come in after a few minutes of being out there alone."

So, we went over the pros and cons of the correction collar for about fifteen minutes when Amber suddenly burst through the door, breathing heavily and carrying a plastic pitcher she had found outside. Tucked neatly inside were the blooming weeds she had been picking earlier.

She ran over to Peggy and handed them to her gallantly.

"These are for you for Mother's Day," she said, a twinkle of mischief in her eyes. "I know it's not Mother's Day, but I wanted you to have them early."

Peggy beamed, thanking her and giving her a hug. I thought to myself, *Uhhhh… this little girl has an agenda for these flowers. I am sure of it.*

True to my child psychology degree, I didn't have to wait long. While Amber was flipping in the kitchen, trying to do handstands,

Peggy pleaded, "Amber, please stop. It's distracting me from what Alisa and I are talking about."

Amber's face shifted into that defiant look that every parent knows all too well. "I don't have to. Why don't you make me? Na-na-na-na-na! That's what I thought, because you can't," she laughed.

She did another handstand, and Peggy looked at me and shrugged her shoulders. "I think I need a shock collar for Amber, too!" she joked

"That's not going to happen because I will just kick you every time you shock me! Ha! Ha! Ha!" Amber shot back confidently.

That was it.

"Alisa Pause," as I jokingly call my menopause, kicked in.

I couldn't take it anymore.

"Why would you talk to your grandmother that way after just giving her those beautiful flowers?" I said, verbatim. "That was rude. I think you should apologize to her right now. She has given you a wonderful place to live, a room fit for a princess. She loves you and takes good care of you."

"I don't care because she deserves it. She shouldn't tell me what to do," Amber replied while doing another handstand.

I looked at Peggy. She looked back at me with silent acknowledgment.

"Alright, young lady. You are now grounded from your video games for two weeks," Peggy said, winking at me.

All hell broke loose. Amber began screaming and crying, yelling that she hated her grandmother. She even yelled that she wished Peggy were dead. That was honestly it for me.

I saw red.

"So, if you hate her so much," I said, grabbing the pitcher of weeds, "I am going to take those flowers and throw them away. Your grandmother does not even want them anymore. Why would she want flowers from someone who hates her? I know I wouldn't. So let me have those flowers." I walked toward the table.

Amber snatched them up, ran to her bedroom, jumped on her bed, and threw the covers over herself.

I looked at Peggy. She gave me the *I know* look.

I went into the bedroom and pulled the covers off her.

"Amber, you need to give me those flowers right now," I said firmly.

"No!!! I don't have to!" she yelled, clutching them tightly.

"I am going to count to three, and you had better put them on your nightstand," Peggy commanded. "One... two..."

Before she could say three, Amber quickly placed them on the nightstand. "When I get ungrounded, I am going to take those flowers back and keep them for myself," she muttered.

I politely maneuvered Peggy out of the way, walked around the bed, and picked up the flowers.

"You don't have to worry about that because I am throwing them away. Come with me... come on..." I said, taking Amber's hand and leading her into the kitchen.

As we walked, we passed Mee Mee, still silently lurking in the corner between the living room and the kitchen. I took Amber to the trash can and dumped the flowers inside, pushing them down deep beneath the other garbage.

Amber tried to pull away from me and lunge into the trash, but she couldn't manage it.

I closed the lid.

"If I hear about you digging those flowers back out of the trash, the next time I come over, it won't be to take Maggie to doggie boot camp; it will be to take you. And trust me, you don't want that," I said, attempting to put just enough fear in her.

"I will have you picking up all the dog poop, digging up dirt to fill every hole the dogs have made, sleeping in a kennel with blankets, eating one meal a day of my choice, whether you like it or not. AND if you are not transformed in three weeks, I will keep you for another three."

I kid you not, Amber stood there looking me dead in the eyes, contemplating it as if she were actually entertaining the thought of going.

Peggy looked at me and said, "She is actually giving it some thought."

Amber suddenly took off running to her room, dove onto her bed, pulled the covers over herself, and started rolling all over it until she tumbled right off onto the floor. There was a slight pause, but quickly she started rolling again, screaming at the top of her lungs.

"Well, I guess I am going to head home now," I said, loud enough for Amber to hear. "Do not get those flowers out of the trash. I promise you don't want to do that."

Amber just kept screaming and rolling across the floor.

Peggy smiled at me and said, "She needed you as much as Maggie."

"I wish I could move in and solve all your problems, but you know…" I replied.

We laughed lightly and walked toward the front door.

As we stood there, Peggy began recapping Maggie's daily routine. She told me she had been tying Maggie up in the garage at night because she had become destructive. Maggie had been lying quietly on the floor beside her husband the entire time all of this was going on. I had noticed how she stayed low, out of the line of fire, observing everything. What a smart girl she was, possibly even trying to comfort Peggy's husband.

I explained that tying her up could be adding to her frustration and creating even more unwanted behavior. I told Peggy that Maggie should be on a routine and kept in a crate at night rather than tied up. I gave her examples of dogs who developed frustration and aggression, even though they were not naturally aggressive.

Then, out of nowhere, her husband began to cry. He yelled out in a slurred, trembling voice, "Tie a dog up for seven years… seven years… with no hope. Why? Why would I do that? Why?"

He was trembling, his hands jerking back and forth. Peggy ignored it at first, until I asked gently, "Is he okay?"

She rushed over to him. "Honey, are you okay? Do you need anything?"

Astonishingly, he responded.

"No… I am okay. I… I… I am okay."

His arms held that waxy flexibility I had seen before in mentally ill patients in a stupor. Peggy gently maneuvered his arms back down, and he stopped crying. Then he returned to watching television as if nothing had happened.

Peggy gently maneuvered his arms back down, and the crying stopped. He returned to staring at the television as if nothing had ever happened.

Peggy turned back to me, tears in her eyes. "He was responding to what we were talking about, wasn't he? That is the first time he has answered me back in a year."

I was looking at Maggie, who placed her front paws softly onto his lap while he stroked her head once.

I was completely thrown by his reaction, already accustomed to the fact that he didn't speak or respond. Maggie tried to comfort him, and seeing his reaction as he stroked her hair was unforgettable.

It was as if they understood one another telepathically.

Maggie, the terrorist, suddenly became the ally in all of this for him. What a spectacular view of her I had, front-row seats to a transformation that was absolutely amazing. It even brought tears to my eyes as I looked back at Peggy.

"Yes," I told softly. "He undoubtedly responded to what we were talking about. Did he tie a dog up at one time?"

"Yes," Peggy said. "He tied a beloved Beagle up for about seven years to keep him from running off. He took him to work and on hikes in the woods on a leash because he felt so bad about keeping him tied. That dog died about six months before he became ill. He was devastated, but he never said he regretted tying him up. This is the first time I have ever heard him express that."

How remarkable for me to experience this firsthand.

I explained to Peggy that I would return to show her how to use the correction collar once she had purchased one, and told her to call me. As I prepared to leave, Maggie walked up to me and gave me her paw mid-air, I guess to say goodbye. I took her paw and shook it.

Just as I reached the door, Amber came running out of her room and asked when I would be back.

"I will probably be back in a week," I said. "So, you better be on your best behavior, okay?"

As she kicked up into a handstand, she replied, "Okay."

I walked over to Peggy's husband and leaned down toward him.

"We won't tie Maggie up anymore. I promise you."

His eyes followed me as I stood up, though he never moved his head. He gazed at me with what felt like distrust.

"Peggy," I said gently but firmly, "we won't tie Maggie up anymore, right? We are going to put her in a comfortable bed with blankets, right?"

"Yes," she replied. "We will put her in a bed with blankets. She will be more comfortable, and I will take the cord out of the garage."

His eyes drifted back to the television, and that was it.

Mee Mee was standing by the fireplace in front of us, quietly lurking, never opening her mouth to utter a single word.

I left with Amber giving me a huge hug goodbye. It was almost as if she needed someone to give her structure and lines that she could not cross. Maggie needed the very same thing, ironically.

* * *

Two weeks later, I travelled back to Peggy's home. The home dynamics were largely the same, yet the atmosphere had shifted. Amber was more complacent, and Mee Mee was asleep on the couch.

Maggie was not barking or backing away; instead, she greeted me by offering her paw. This time, she seemed ready, almost as if she anticipated the changes that were needed.

I noticed Peggy's husband following me with his eyes as I moved around the room. I truly believe that somewhere in his locked-up mind, he knew exactly what was going on around him. Two red-headed teenage boys were sitting on the living room floor this time; Amber ran over to tell me they were her cousins.

"Amber," I asked, "did you get those flowers out of the trash after I left the other day?"

"Nope! I left them there, didn't I, Grandma?"

"She sure did," Peggy said with pride. "She even came off her grounding early for good behavior."

I praised Amber for a few moments, then prompted Peggy and Amber to step outside so I could work some magic on Maggie.

We all went outside to the backyard, where Peggy had recently installed fencing since my last visit.

"This is awesome, Peggy. Now she can run and expend some of that pent-up energy," I said, genuinely impressed.

"I have been putting her in a crate at night and have not tied her up anymore," Peggy said with a laugh. "You know, since you were here, Maggie's behavior has been much better for some reason. Maybe I am just hoping she is,"

"We will see about that, won't we?" I replied.

I turned the collar on and placed it around Maggie's neck. She immediately took off running through the yard.

"Amber, take off running so I can correct Maggie," I instructed.

Amber ran, and true to form, Maggie sprinted after her. Just as Maggie jumped to knock her down, I activated the vibration warning. Maggie stopped for a second, startled by the strange sensation and the high-pitched beep.

"Amber, take off again! Jump around and swing your arms this time," I said, wanting to get Maggie fully worked up again.

Amber took off, swinging her arms, and Maggie went into a dead run after her. Just as she jumped to knock Amber down, I gave the warning again, followed by a shock. Maggie yelped and ran straight to the back door of the house.

I had Amber continue running and singing loudly, but Maggie would not budge from that back door. One time was all it took for her to get the correction.

I left that day hopeful that this was finally the ticket for Peggy to manage her household.

As I was walking out, Peggy joked, "Hey, do they make shock collars for children? Because I still need one for Amber."

"No, they don't!" Amber exclaimed. "But I have been doing better, haven't I, Grandma?"

Peggy affirmed her with a smile.

"Let me know how things are going," I told her as I walked to my car. "And if I need to come back to help, you know I don't mind making another trip."

* * *

About a week later, I called Peggy. The correction collar was working perfectly. She had only needed to give Maggie a couple of corrections since I left.

Maggie is a working-class breed, and unfortunately, some breeds require far more structure and purpose than the average owner can provide. If I had my way in this situation, I would have rehomed her to a farm where she could work cattle and fulfill her natural instincts. However, I handled the situation the best I could under the circumstances.

Maggie is deeply loved by this family, and I hope they can coexist peacefully for many years to come.

Successful Dogs in training and their owners

"Training starts here, success ends with you!"

— Alisa Peterson-White

JUPITER

Jupiter is an amazing German Shepherd (GSD). He came to train with me two years ago when he was just a year old. At that time, his owner, Troy Pope, M.D., had been working with him and had already taught him to sit and lie down. However, his primary issues were behavioral; Jupiter believed he was the "alpha."

He was jumping on people, pulling horribly on the leash, and selectively listening to commands only when he felt like it. After completing my three-week boot camp, his behavior changed significantly. He no longer challenged authority or viewed himself as the alpha. His obedience became flawless, his leash pulling was corrected, and the jumping stopped entirely.

That being said, the reason I consider Jupiter such a success story isn't just what he accomplished here; it's how Troy maintained the training at home. Troy hikes five to ten miles with him almost every day, follows through with obedience daily, and consistently keeps Jupiter's attitude in check.

As a traveling E.R. doctor, Troy passes through my area twice a month. For two years, Jupiter has continued to board with me, and we are now working on advanced obedience, which he is handling magnificently. When an owner takes training seriously, the results are wonderful. I am so proud of Jupiter and Dr. Troy Pope!

TAKODA

Takoda came to me for training about five years ago. What made him so special was that he was completely deaf. His owner, Brynlee Bigalow, was a college freshman at the time and was desperate to find a way to communicate with him. Takoda was not unruly; in fact, he was quite well-mannered, but Brynlee simply didn't know how to get him to respond to commands like sit, stay, down, and heel without sound.

While Brynlee was away on vacation with her family, she boarded Takoda with me and asked if I could teach him a few commands. Training dogs in sign language has become one of my specialties, and I absolutely love working with hearing-impaired dogs. They soak up the training like a sponge; up until that moment, they've had no way to understand their humans or "talk" back.

I taught Takoda basic commands along with behavioral cues like "off," "drop it," "leave it," and "happy" (my sign for "good boy"). He performed amazingly, as hearing-impaired dogs often do once the communication gap is bridged. When Brynlee returned to pick him up, she was thrilled beyond words. Before they left, we had her work with Takoda for a while; he watched her every hand signal and completed every task she asked of him perfectly.

It was truly a beautiful moment. Tragically, not long after, Brynlee was involved in a car accident on a terrible rainy night; she was ejected from the vehicle and passed away. I was traveling in San Francisco when I heard the news and was completely devastated. I could not wrap my mind around such a tragedy.

My husband and I are close friends with her parents; I even went to school with her father. Although her parents admitted they were "cat people," they didn't hesitate to keep Takoda.

While her father was reluctant at first, he has faithfully kept up with all of Takoda's training, ensuring he gets plenty of walks and exercise. We have continued to board Takoda several times a year throughout this time. He remains one of the most well-adjusted, well-mannered, and well-behaved dogs I have seen in a very long time. Thanks to his owners for maintaining his structure at home, he has a very loving and happy life.

STELLA

Stella, a German Shepherd (GSD), came to me for a behavioral boot camp over a year ago due to aggression. She had been lunging and barking on the leash at every person who passed her or entered her home. She also had a history of biting, though the circumstances were somewhat "questionable."

The incident occurred in the owner's basement while her son had friends over. They were hanging out, getting loud, and running around. The owner was not entirely sure what triggered the shift, but Stella suddenly lunged at one of the friends and bit him. Stella had been raised by the family since she was a puppy; she was now two years old, and the aggressive behavior had only started about six months before her owner, Maria Jayme-Martin, contacted me for help.

When they arrived at my office for the drop-off, the tension was immediate. As Maria was busy filling out the intake paperwork, I stepped out from behind my counter to ask her a question. Stella didn't hesitate; she charged at me twice.

I stood my ground without backing up, and Stella did not like the challenge. The third time she lunged, she bit me in the stomach. I never changed my stance or my demeanor. I could tell it was a guarding reflex mixed with fear-based aggression, and I knew in that moment I was going to have my hands full.

After Maria left, I was able to lead Stella on the leash to get her weight and settle her into a large kennel. I gave her a couple of hours to decompress before approaching her again, hoping she would be calmer. Eventually, I was able to get her out and into the yard to run with the other dogs; she did absolutely fine with both me and the pack.

Stella stayed with me for six weeks to work through her aggression. A few days before she was scheduled to go home, I took her to several dog-friendly public stores. She was unsure at first when passing strangers, but a slight snap of the leash was all it took to redirect her, and she calmed down quickly.

We visited four different stores that day, and she was amazing. She never lunged, pulled, barked, or growled at anyone. In the last store, the cashier asked if she could give Stella a treat. After giving the clerk a quick overview of our progress, I felt confident enough to let them interact. The clerk came around the counter and offered the treat; Stella took it calmly and even allowed the clerk to pet her. **Success!**

What Stella truly needed was to build her confidence and learn to trust me as her leader. She began to follow my direction, knowing that if I signaled a person was "okay," she could relax. By stepping into that leadership role, I took a huge weight off her shoulders, allowing her to stop worrying and just be a happy dog.

Her owner, Maria, now works with Stella daily. She takes her for walks, redirects her when necessary, and maintains her obedience training. Because of this consistency, Stella has learned to trust Maria implicitly. If Maria says a person is good, Stella accepts them.

I am incredibly proud of Stella and how far this training has taken her. She has boarded with me many times over the past year and continues to do amazingly well. Congratulations to Maria and Stella for their dedication and for following through with the hard work at home!

SUMMARY

WHAT THE DOGS HAVE TAUGHT ME

All of these stories are meant to help you understand a simple truth: as owners, we are often the ones who create most of a dog's worst behaviors. By not allowing a dog to simply *be a dog*. By treating them as a human or family member rather than as a dog. By letting family dynamics and household chaos spill over onto them. By lack of time and dedication to their dog.  Not giving proper corrections. Not maintaining structure and order.

By not teaching obedience. By failing to work dogs of the working-class breeds. Not challenging the minds of truly intelligent dogs with games. In my thirty-five years of training, these are some of the things I have witnessed with owners.

Every dog trainer has their own unique twist to their methods, shining in some areas more than others. I personally love and specialize in behavioral modification.

I began this journey as a little girl, spending summers with my grandfather on his farm in Jackson, Tennessee. My grandfather was not a "dog trainer" by trade, but he was an exceptional dog handler. He understood all of his animals on that farm, even the deer we would sneak out to watch in the early mornings.

He taught me how animals think and how they process the world around them. He took a special interest in how naturally training dogs came to me. Together, we trained a horse, cats, and even ducks, but dogs became my favorite.

So much of my grandfather lives on in my training methods today. Back in those days, people often used very harsh corrections with animals; methods handed down through generations by their grandparents and parents. I remember my grandfather once took a Beagle out to hunt rabbits. Instead, the Beagle chased a cat up a tree. In response, he shot the cat and tied it to the dog for two days. The beagle never chased another cat for as long as he lived.

Obviously, this is something no one would do in today's dog-training world, with our growing love and respect for dogs. However, what he truly taught me was not cruelty, but the importance of reading a dog's body language, of looking into their eyes to see their inner soul. To know what they are thinking and saying through their posture, their movement, and what you read deep within their eyes.

I take great pride in being able to look into a dog's eyes and know if they are sick, depressed, anxious, abused, or happy. Dogs talk to me. They tell me what they are feeling. Dogs talk to me. They tell me what they are feeling. My grandfather had a gift for listening to the silent language of animals, and I like to think he passed that gift on to me.

When a dog is completely out of control, jumping repeatedly, play-biting, growling at the owner, becoming possessive of objects or food, ignoring commands, humping family members and the list goes in; it is a handling and guidance error on the part of the owners.

The dog needs direction, pack orientation within the family, proper corrections, stability, and both physical and mental exercise. A dog needs clear boundaries. He needs to understand what behavior is acceptable and what is not. Just like children, dogs need guidance, correction, consistency, and structure.

It never ceases to amaze me how many owners allow their dogs to develop such inappropriate behaviors. I have seen owners in tears, not knowing how things became so out of control. I have seen the exact same thing with parents of children.

And the line I hear most often:

"I don't know what to do anymore. I GIVE UP. I have tried everything, and nothing works."

It truly is not that the owners do not care, rather they do not have the proper skill sets to guide their dogs properly.

I have also met many owners who believe their dog thinks and feels exactly as they do. For example, an owner may be upset about leaving their dog at a facility while they go on vacation, and say:

"My dog will think I abandoned them and that I don't love them."

The truth is, the dog may be somewhat confused because they are out of their routine, but they are mainly confused about the energy that the owner is giving off to them.

When an owner confidently drops off their dog, gives a quick pet, and leaves, the dog remains calm and quickly learns the new routines. However, when an owner lingers, hugging the dog in tears, the dog struggles to adjust. The dog has a difficult time accepting new people and new dogs, and often shows signs of depression. The dog is upset because the owner is upset, sad, uncertain, and lacking confidence in their decision to leave. When the owner leaves without worry, the dog is eager, happy, and adjusts easily.

Dogs do not think in "gray areas" or layers of complex emotion. Just as they do not know how long they are being left at a facility. Whether it is one day or nine days, they do not have any concept. Owners often believe their dogs are counting the days while staying at a facility. The dogs are not. They live in the present moment.

Owners have also said to me, "I have to give my dog a bite of everything I eat. If I don't, my dog gets mad at me and pouts. He won't have anything to do with me for the rest of the day."

It is possible that the dog may be a little upset because the owner has taught them to expect that bite of food. When you do not give it, the dog is confused and wonders why. They may even think they are being punished for something they have not done. More often, though, it is a learned behavior because the owner rewards the dog afterward with extra love and apologies, feeling guilty. The dog learns that ignoring the owner leads to attention and maybe even an extra treat.

Dogs learn through association. This is the key to understanding them and knowing the proper type of corrections or directions to use. Never make the mistake of believing a dog is thinking about these situations the way a human does. They are simply responding to learned associations and the outcomes they have experienced.

When you hear people say that a dog takes on the owner's personality, there is truth to that concept. Owners who are highly anxious often have untrained dogs that display anxious behaviors, leading to destruction, excessive barking, or nervous habits.

If an owner is scattered and hyperactive, the dog may mirror that energy with zooming, jumping, escaping, or running away. If an owner struggles with anger, the dog may become unbalanced, even attacking a stranger on the street without provocation.

Dogs are incredibly perceptive. They absorb the emotional climate of the home.

Let me give you an example of five well-behaved, balanced dogs and the personality behind them.

I personally own five dogs of varying breeds: a Frug (French Bulldog/Pug mix), a French Bulldog, two black Labrador Retrievers, and a Great Pyrenees.

A few years ago, I switched veterinarians and had him come out to my home and facility to administer their yearly vaccinations.

He started with my house dogs: the Frug and the French Bulldog. When he finished, he played and loved on them both and said, "What sweet dogs, so friendly." He then moved on to my black Labradors, petting them and remarking, "They are so laid-back and gentle-natured. Such sweet dogs."

Finally, he approached my Pyrenees, who does not take to strangers easily, which is true to the breed. He spoke to her softly as he came closer. She became a little nervous stirring around in circles but I reassured her: "It's OK, Alpha. He will not hurt you." I sent her calming energy, and she allowed him to pet her and give the vaccinations without incident. When he finished, she leaned her head into him, asking for love again.

The veterinarian leaned back, clearly impressed.

"Wow," he said. "Your dogs all have such sweet, loving personalities. So well behaved, and Alpha calmed down as quickly as you told her to."

"Do you know what this says to me? Not only are you a dog trainer, but you are an exceptional dog owner. These dogs are a product of *you*. It also tells me a lot about you as a person."

Naturally, I was curious. "What exactly does it tell you about me?" I asked.

I was already running through different interpretations in my mind. Does he think I am overbearing? Does he think I am too much of a drill sergeant? Maybe he thinks I am too hard on them, or maybe he believes they are afraid of me and behave simply because they know I will correct them if they act out.

To the contrary, he smiled and said:

"You are calm with them. You have obviously taught them emotional stability and given them proper direction. They definitely trust you and know you would never put them in a sketchy situation. They are emotionally balanced, which tells me you are too.

"You are not harsh, but you are firm. You are not abusive, but you accept only the best behaviors. They are loving, and so are you. They follow your guidance, which tells me you are a great pack leader.

"Honestly, I wish every client of mine understood dogs the way you obviously do. Do you train every dog that comes here the same way you have trained your own?"

Without hesitation I said, "Of course! I love every dog I am lucky enough to work with."

He grinned and said, "You have my vote!"

Over the years, he has continued to send clients to me with out-of-control dogs. Later, when I visit his office, he tells me how his job is continuing to be much easier now with well-balanced dogs and owners.

This was simply the best example I could give you, and I am certainly not trying to build up your perception for me solely. Rather, I hope it illustrates how important it is for owners to change their own behaviors.

When I work with an owner who struggles with anxiety, hyperactivity, or depression, it is imperative that I also address the owner's issues. This is where my psychology degree becomes intricate in the process. When my veterinarian says that his clients are balanced as well as their dogs, it makes me feel that I have helped heal the entire family unit.

If a dog trainer only looks at the dog's behavior without factoring in the dynamics and energy of the household, the approach will fail. A trainer can teach the dog, but if the dog returns to the same environment, regression is inevitable. Owners must understand that change begins within themselves before they can expect proper behavior from their dog.

I do not sit down for counseling sessions with owners, nor do I help them through divorces or childhood trauma. What I do is explain how their emotions are affecting their dog's behavior. To truly help the dog, they must regroup and rethink their own behavior.

This shift miraculously changes both the owner and the dog. It is amazing to watch the transformations that take place. When people cannot figure out their own emotions, they often will for their dog.

That is my reward.

LAKE CUMBERLAND K-9 TRAINING CENTER

PHOTO GALLERY, ALISA PETERSON-WHITE, 35+ YEARS OF PROFESSIONAL DOG TRAINING

Classroom Visit

LCK-9 Has Trained Over 5000 Dogs!

We Love Each and Every Dog

Alisa Paterson-White

LCK-9 Training Center

Bench Buddies at Rest

Live, Love, Bark

Alisa's personal Dog 'Alpha'

Adorable Pitbull Puppy

Patches - Graduation Day

Two Dogs in Perfect Sit-Stay

Blue - Proud LCK-9 Graduate

Tiny Yorkie with Art

Two Dogs Sleeping Peacefully

Dog Graduation Achievement

Dog Peeking Through Cat Flap

A pair of quick learners on the mat.

A peaceful rest after a busy day.

A unique look for a unique
dog

Resting but Alert

Adorable Duo on Display

Labrador in Training

Holiday Spirit at the Rocky
Hollow Athletic Centre

Festive Pups, Joyful Hearts

Christmas Celebration with
K-9 Family at Nursing Home

Blue-Eyed Pup on the Mat

Alert Dog Sitting Indoors

Cavapoo in a nice Sit-Stay

Golden Retriever & Rottweiler Together

Stella Sitting Calmly

Stella in a palm/stay

Takoda learning down in sign language

Takoda learning sit in sign language

Alisa's Grandfather

Golden Retriever in Training

GSD with Flopped Ear

Cross-Species Companionship

Pack Orientation Training

Poodle Mix & French Bulldog

Focused Pup Pair in Sweaters

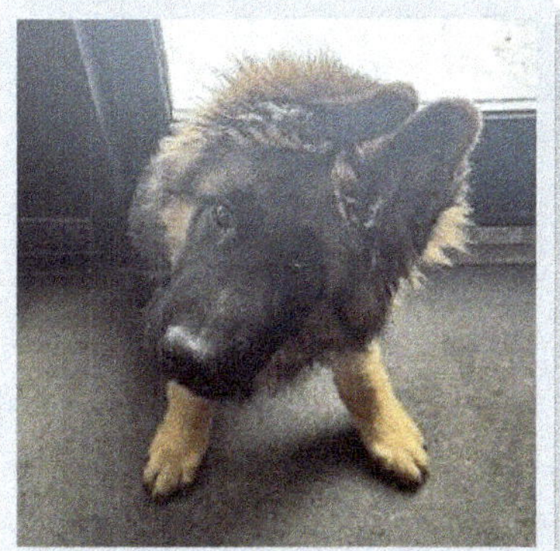

Attentive Shepherd Indoors

Different Breeds, Same Lesson

Siberian Husky in Training Indoors

Building Discipline Together

Puppy Learning Leash Control

Dog with Heterochromia

Young Pup Practicing Sit-Stay

Obedience Practice for Power Breeds

Alisa with Her Two Labs

GSD Practicing Down-Stay in Public

Alisa and Lake Cumberland K-9 Companions

Relaxed Shepherd Beside its owner

Family Bond Behind the
Training Center

Alisa and Art Exploring Together

Family Journey, Shared Milestone

The Language of the Pack
with Alisa

Alisa and Shih Tzu

Celebrating Our Recent K-9
Graduates

APPENDIX A

QUICK REFERENCE GUIDE

Common Problems and Solutions

1. Jumping on People

The Problem: Your dog jumps on you, guests, or strangers to greet them.

Why It Happens: Lack of discipline, seeking attention, excitement, or testing boundaries.

The Solution: Never allow jumping. Turn your back immediately when the dog jumps. Use the "Off!" command firmly. Put the dog in a down/stay as a consequence. Only give attention when all four paws are on the ground. Be consistent, every single time.

2. Destructive Chewing

The Problem: Your dog chews furniture, shoes, walls, or other household items.

Why It Happens: Boredom, lack of exercise, separation anxiety, insufficient mental stimulation, or lack of structure.

The Solution: Provide appropriate chew toys. Exercise the dog physically (walks, backpack work for working breeds). Exercise the dog mentally (obedience training, learning tricks, problem-solving games). Catch them in the act and correct immediately; after-the-fact corrections do not work. Establish clear leadership. Working breeds must have jobs.

3. House Training Issues / Marking

The Problem: The dog urinates or defecates in the house despite being house-trained.

Why It Happens: Medical issues, incomplete training, territorial marking (especially unneutered males), anxiety, or lack of routine.

The Solution: Rule out medical issues first. Catch the behavior in the act and correct immediately with a firm "No!" followed by taking the dog outside. Use crate training at night. Establish a consistent feeding schedule and bathroom routine. For attention-seeking or anxiety-related urination, address the underlying need for structure and stability. Neuter males who are marking.

4. Excessive Barking

The Problem: The dog barks constantly, at people, other dogs, noises, or seemingly nothing.

Why It Happens: Territorial behavior, attention-seeking, boredom, anxiety, or lack of socialization.

The Solution: Identify the trigger. For attention-seeking barking, ignore it completely. For territorial barking, calmly redirect and establish boundaries. Teach the "Quiet!" command. Interrupt the behavior if necessary (a noise interrupter can help redirect attention). Provide sufficient physical and mental exercise.

5. Aggression (Toward People or Dogs)

The Problem: The dog growls, snaps, or bites at people or other dogs.

Why It Happens: Fear, lack of socialization, anxiety, resource guarding, or feeling threatened.

The Solution: This is serious; seek professional help immediately. Work in controlled environments for socialization. Address triggers calmly and consistently. For food aggression, implement structured feeding routines (sit/stay before meals). Never ignore or excuse aggressive behavior.

6. Separation Anxiety

The Problem: The dog becomes destructive, vocal, or distressed when left alone.

Why It Happens: Lack of independence training, inconsistent routines, anxiety, or over-dependence.

The Solution: Leave calmly without emotional goodbyes. Avoid making departures or returns dramatic. Practice leaving for short periods and gradually increase duration. Crate training can help. Reinforce obedience and structure. Your energy must remain calm and confident.

7. Herding Behavior / Nipping

The Problem: The dog nips at heels or hands or attempts to "herd" family members.

Why It Happens: Breed instinct (common in herding breeds such as Australian Shepherds, Border Collies, and Heelers) that is not being properly channeled.

The Solution: Provide an appropriate outlet for the herding instinct. Give them structured tasks or activities. Obedience training adds structure. Redirect the behavior to acceptable activities. Correct firmly and immediately if the dog nips people. Working breeds must be mentally and physically engaged, or they will create their own job.

The Alpha Checklist

Ask yourself these questions honestly:

- Does your dog eat before you do? (They should eat after.)

- Does your dog decide when the walk ends?

- Does your dog sleep in your bed and take the prime position?

- Do you change your plans or tiptoe around your dog's moods?

- Do you make lengthy emotional goodbyes when leaving the house?

- Do you give your dog treats simply for existing, not for performing a command?

- Does your dog jump on guests, and you laugh or call it "friendly"?

- Do you allow your dog to ignore commands without consequences?

If you answered yes to more than three of these, your dog is likely running your household. The good news: this is fixable.

Breed Research: Know Before You Commit

Before bringing any dog home, research these key questions:

- What was this breed originally designed to do? (herding, hunting, protection, companionship)

- How much daily exercise does this breed require?

- How much mental stimulation does this breed need?

- Does this breed have strong prey, herding, or guarding instincts?

- Is this breed known for stubbornness or ease of training?

- Does this breed do well in apartments or need space?

- What are the common health issues for this breed?

Matching the right breed to your lifestyle is one of the single most important decisions you will make as a dog owner. Do not choose a dog based on looks alone.

APPENDIX B

TRAINING TERMINOLOGY GLOSSARY

These are terms you will encounter in dog training discussions, along with how I personally apply and understand them from 35 years of hands-on experience.

Alpha (Pack Leader)

The individual within a group who establishes the rules, maintains order, and leads the rest. In a household, you must be the alpha. When you abdicate this role, your dog will step into it by default, often with disastrous results.

Association Learning

Dogs learn primarily through association: they connect an action with an outcome. This is why timing is critical in corrections and rewards. A dog can only associate a reward or correction with what they are doing in that precise moment, not something that happened five minutes ago.

Correction

A response to unwanted behavior that communicates to the dog that the behavior is unacceptable. It is not the same as punishment. A correction should be immediate, appropriate to the behavior, and followed by showing the dog what they *should* do instead.

Crate Training

Using a crate as a dog's personal "den" for safety, housebreaking, and creating a calm resting space. When done correctly, a dog views their crate as a sanctuary, not a punishment. Never use a crate punitively.

Desensitization

Gradually exposing a dog to a stimulus that causes anxiety or aggression, at a level low enough not to trigger a reaction, until they become comfortable with it. This is used for dogs that are fearful of specific sounds, objects, or situations.

Down-Stay

A command requiring the dog to lie down and remain in that position until released. This is a calm, controlled position that reinforces focus and leadership. Start with short durations and gradually increase the time.

Drive

A dog's innate instinct or motivation: prey drive, play drive, food drive, etc. Understanding a dog's drives is essential to training them effectively and preventing frustration behaviors.

Feral Pack

Wild or semi-wild dogs living and surviving together in a pack. They demonstrate natural canine instincts and social structures without human interference. Studying feral packs can provide insight into instinctual canine behavior.

Flood Therapy

An exposure technique where a dog is exposed to a fear stimulus at full intensity to break the fear response. This is a professional technique and should never be attempted without expert guidance, as it can backfire catastrophically.

Food Aggression / Resource Guarding

When a dog becomes possessive or aggressive around food, toys, or other valued items. This behavior reflects insecurity or perceived competition over resources and must be addressed promptly through structured training.

Heel

A command requiring the dog to walk directly beside the handler, matching the handler's pace, on a loose leash. The heel position physically puts the dog at your side, not out front, reinforcing that you lead.

Humanizing

Treating a dog as if they are human by attributing human emotions, reasoning, or motivations to them. This can lead to behavioral problems because dogs communicate and process the world differently than humans.

Negative Reinforcement

In behavioral science, negative reinforcement means removing an unpleasant stimulus to increase desired behavior. However, many people mistakenly use the term to describe giving attention to bad behavior. Dogs will repeat behaviors that receive attention, even if it is yelling or scolding, because attention can reinforce the behavior.

Obsessive-Compulsive Behaviors

Repetitive behaviors such as excessive licking, chasing lights, spinning, or tail-chasing. These often indicate anxiety, frustration, lack of stimulation, or unmet needs. Intelligent and high-energy dogs are especially prone if under-stimulated.

Omega

The lowest-ranking member of a pack. In a well-structured household, no dog should feel like the Omega in a way that causes suffering, but all dogs should understand they rank below the humans in the household.

Pack Mentality

The natural tendency of canines to function within a structured social hierarchy with clear roles, rules, and leadership. All domestic dogs retain this instinct regardless of breed or upbringing.

Positive Reinforcement

Rewarding desired behavior with treats, praise, play, or affection. This is a highly effective and evidence-based component of training. Dogs are more likely to repeat behaviors that produce positive outcomes.

Recall

The ability to call a dog back to you reliably. A solid recall is one of the most important safety commands a dog can know, and one of the most commonly neglected. Practice first in controlled, low-distraction environments before progressing to more challenging settings.

Redirect

Interrupting an unwanted behavior and guiding the dog toward an acceptable alternative. Example: redirecting a chewing dog from your furniture to a chew toy.

Regression

When a dog returns to previously corrected unwanted behaviors. This usually occurs due to inconsistency, lack of reinforcement, changes in routine, or unclear expectations.

Separation Anxiety

Distress when separated from the owner. This can stem from over-dependence, inconsistent boundaries, lack of independence training, or environmental changes. Gradual independence-building and structured routines help reduce it.

Sit/Stay

A command for the dog to sit and remain seated until released. A foundational obedience skill that builds focus, impulse control, and structure.

Socialization

Exposing a dog to a wide variety of people, dogs, environments, sounds, and situations during their development so they learn to navigate the world with confidence rather than fear or aggression.

Submission

When a dog displays calming or appeasing signals toward another dog or human. Signs may include lowering the head, avoiding direct eye contact, rolling onto the back, or a relaxed body posture. Submission is not the same as fear; it can also indicate trust and social communication.

Time-Out

A calm, neutral consequence for inappropriate behavior where the dog is briefly removed from stimulation (such as being placed in a crate or down/stay). It should not be emotional or angry. The goal is to show that inappropriate behavior ends access to attention or activity.

Working-Class Breed

Breeds originally developed to perform specific tasks: herding, hunting, guarding, tracking, or pulling. These breeds require purposeful work and structured outlets, or they will create their own "jobs," usually destructive ones.

ACKNOWLEDGEMENTS

I will never be able to express how amazing my grandfather, Alfred Peterson, truly was. He was such a gentle soul; as a child, I can recall only one instance where I saw him truly upset. He was so in tune with animals that he seemed to share an unspoken language with them. It was astonishing to watch him communicate with his cows, dogs, chickens, and old barn cats without a single word; it was as if they could read his mind.

I believe they learned his body language, his movements, and his energy to know exactly what he wanted. If he needed the cows to move to another pasture, he would simply say a specific word, and they would gather and move collectively.

My father once told me a story about my grandfather walking through the pasture one evening when he accidentally stepped into a large hole and fell. All the cows gathered around him, bellowing with worry, until he stood up and said, "I'm okay," in his gentle voice. Just like that, they went back to grazing. I memorized everything he did with animals to the best of my ability; I was a sponge waiting to soak up every drop of his wisdom.

I am everything I have become with animals because of him. Though I have dedicated my life to studying animal behavior, I still feel I fall short of the natural gift he possessed. Even though he has passed on, I feel him watching over me with pride. He is a strong voice inside of me and my primary drive. Thank you, Papa Peterson, for honoring me with your knowledge and encouragement. I dedicate my success in dog training and this book to your loving memory. You have been missed every single day of the forty years since you left me.

Thirty years ago, I walked into a veterinarian's office in Somerset, Kentucky, and spotted a corkboard covered in business cards and lost dog flyers. Tucked among them was a dog trainer's number. I took it down and called as soon as I got home. His name was James Waters, and we became instant friends. He helped me work my Golden Retriever at a professional level, and she passed her training with flying colors. But James kept telling me I should consider a career in the field myself.

During one of our last classes together, he pulled me aside and said, "Alisa, you have such a natural ability with dogs. You should really think about changing your career. You have a psychology background that gives you an edge in understanding their behavior. I truly believe you would be a great success." I told him about my grandfather and how he had nurtured that ability in me. James then offered to mentor me in the AKC standard of training. It took me a couple of weeks to decide, but I eventually took the dive.

I spent over five years apprenticing under James. We held countless obedience classes, worked with the dogs he would board and train. We spent hours upon hours talking on the phone about dogs and their behaviors. Talking about the temperamental differences within each breed, and yes, I was bitten more times than I would like to admit while learning my breeds.

After my fifth year, I went out on my own, though we continued to work closely on difficult cases. James became a dog trainer during his military service and brought over forty years of experience to our partnership. He is still my go-to when I face a particularly challenging situation. I will never be able to thank him enough for changing the course of my life. James, you are the best, and I am honored to call you both a mentor and a dearest friend.

My husband, Robert Arthur White, has been my supporter, collaborator, and source of encouragement throughout the long process of writing this book. He pushed me when I did not want to write another word, and he read every single story, cheering me on the entire way. Honey, you are my world, and I can never thank you enough for your understanding, patience, and diligence with me. I know I can be a difficult, independent, and complicated woman, yet somehow you find love within the madness as we face each day together.

We cry together, hug and comfort each other when life throws hurdles our way, and find paths over them, just as we do on our many hiking and backpacking adventures. Thank you, honey, for your boundless love. I love and adore you exponentially; you are the warmth of my sunshine.

My final acknowledgement is for my wonderfully idiosyncratic and talented mother, Betty June Withers-Peterson. She passed away five years ago, while I was in the middle of writing this book. While she was able to read some of these pages, she did not live to see them in print. What follows is a letter written directly to her.

LETTER TO MY MOTHER

Mom,

I miss you and long for your presence. A void has settled in my heart, a constant reminder of your absence. I am incomplete, and my heart is forever adrift without you. My love for you is incalculable, measureless, limitless, and eternal.

As a child, you would coerce us kids to read books during the summers and write book reports while our friends were outside frolicking in the fresh air. Thank you for your diligence with us and for widening our perspectives. As a high school student, I was so unsure of myself with each paper I had to write for my English classes. You would sit down with me and my scribbles, guiding me and unlocking my potential. Thank you for turning my insecurity into applicable wisdom.

As a college student, conflicted and battling English Literature, you mentored me through my first semester. You spent hours lying beside me in my bed, encouraging me and proving to me that a mother's love is unselfish. By my second semester, I could hold my own and even unlock interpretations that you yourself had not even conceived. Thank you for your wisdom; your support made a tangible difference in my growth. You are the remarkable miracle of God's tender, guiding hand. Your love has endured long after you let go.

Thank you for supporting me as a dog trainer, even though I knew of your many reservations. As an English Professor, you could not fathom my leaving a psychology degree to work with dogs. You questioned me numerous times whenever we were together. You watched me struggle financially, emotionally, and physically while my own children and I had very little to eat. I understood your trepidation, along with your own internal struggles regarding my determination.

When the hurdles finally became manageable, they did not necessarily disappear, yet I developed the strength, perspective, and resilience to navigate them effectively. I saw your hazed, dimmed eyes transform to sharp crystal. At last, affirmation! You became an immense supporter and delighted in my success. You told me so many times how proud you were of what I had built and overcome.

However, your proudest moment would be twenty-eight years later, as I tackled a book about dog training. You read some of my stories, offering suggestions and changes. You loved many of them, telling me to change nothing. You explained that my stories made you laugh, cry, and ponder, all while learning something with each one. In your words, "It's perfection!"

I am so thankful that you were able to read some of this book. Even though you are in a better place, I have felt your beacon illuminate and continue throughout my process. I want you to know what your youngest son, Keith, said to me after your passing. I thought it was profound, and you should know, as this is how we all felt. Keith wept as he stated, "I walk through stores and navigate through the public as they are smiling, laughing, rushed, and robotic. I think to myself, 'No one knows that the world just took a huge hit, losing our mother. They have no clue.'"

I think when we are grieving so intensely, and our souls are voided temporarily, we innately think that everyone around us is feeling the same way. When you look up and see everyone going on with life as if nothing has changed, we feel isolated within that darkness. Your pack of wolves was grieving, damaged, and suffering; and yes, we were forever wounded. My psychologist once told me that I needed to howl, as the wolves do when losing a pack member. I howl, and I bay daily.

I love you, Mom, and I cannot wait until that meeting in paradise. Rest with the angels, sweet mommy, and know that YOU are my one and only perfection.

I love you,

Alisa

ABOUT THE AUTHOR

I was born in Slidell, Louisiana, in 1967. My dad worked construction on power plants, so we moved quite a bit when I was young. We landed in Somerset, Kentucky, in 1972, and it would become my forever home. We lived in a modest neighborhood where all the kids were friends. We played cops and robbers at night, held wiffle ball tournaments in our backyard, played basketball in neighbors' driveways, and held annual neighborhood picnics. It was a wonderful place to grow up, and I carry so many fond memories of that time.

Every summer, my family took a vacation to my paternal grandparents' farm in Jackson, Tennessee. It was a massive farm where we would swing on tire swings, go fishing in the pond, and pick apples, peaches, and grapes until we were sick. In the evenings after dinner, my grandfather would pick a watermelon from his patch; to this day, it is the best-tasting watermelon I have ever eaten.

During the day, I followed my grandfather everywhere. I was intrigued by his way with animals. He always had several farm dogs, stray cats in the barn, chickens, and a herd of cows. I particularly wanted to spend my time with the dogs. I would teach them tricks like "shake," "high five," and "roll over." My Papa took notice and began teaching me the nuances of the farm. He showed me the differences between the animals and the specific roles of the dogs, explaining why one dog was a natural at herding while another was better suited as a guard dog.

One summer, he had a new terrier mix named JJ. Papa trained JJ to "attack" (playfully) whenever you crooked a finger at him. My grandfather would hold him back while he barked and growled; then, Papa would tell us to run around the house and let him go. JJ would chase us until he caught us. Watching my Papa teach those tricks was my first real lesson in training. By the time I was thirteen, I started training our new Cocker Spaniel puppy. I had him so well-trained that the neighbors took notice and began hiring me to train their dogs. I continued this for years, right up until I married and started having children.

At twenty-seven, I found myself going through a divorce and moving back to Somerset. I had an associate degree in psychology and was in my senior year at Western Kentucky University when I returned home. I began working in the medical field while training dogs on the side. As I was going back to college to finish my psychology degree, I realized that this was not the avenue I wanted to take with my career. I wanted to train dogs full-time, blending my knowledge of psychology with both the dogs and their owners.

After ten years of "slaving away" and barely getting by, I met my husband, Art. My clientele was growing, and I was quickly outgrowing my facility. Art single-handedly built the new facility that I still operate out of today. Now, I receive dogs from all over the United States and the world, almost entirely through word of mouth. Never underestimate the power of a solid reputation in any business.

Running a business has not been without its difficulties. Finding dedicated, reliable employees is a constant challenge, though I have been fortunate to have several phenomenal staff members stay with me for many years, including one who has been with me for over six. However, since COVID-19, finding solid help has become increasingly difficult.

I have also faced the dark side of social media, having been "bashed" online twice. The first time, I won a civil suit where the judge ruled I had done absolutely nothing wrong; the owner was an absolute nut job and ended up in a divorce over his obsession with trying to ruin me.

The second instance involved a woman whose dog got car sick on the way home and threw up a small ball the dog had swallowed. This woman claimed that I had abused, neglected, and taken horrible care of her dog. I eventually confronted her on the phone regarding her Facebook post and the lies she was spreading. When she realized she had no facts to back up her claims, she sputtered, "Uhhhhh... well... explain to me why my dog came home with three gray hairs? She must have been miserable to get those gray hairs!"

In my head, I'm thinking, *You are absolutely crazy.* To provide peace of mind and combat that kind of negativity, I post videos daily of the dogs and puppies so owners can see for themselves that their pets are having a great time. They are well-cared for and have a blast with new friends while receiving the training and direction they need.

Thankfully, my loyal clients flooded her post to defend me, and eventually, the interest fizzled out as she likely moved on to troll someone else. Social media can be your best friend or your worst enemy. Through it all, I stand true to myself, my training, and my absolute love for every one of these dogs.